The Things We Don't Talk About

A Memoir of Hardships, Healing, and Hope

Stacy Bernal

DEDICATION

To my family and my fur babies, the greatest WHY I can think of.

THE THINGS
WE DON'T
TALK ABOUT

ACKNOWLEDGMENTS

There are so many people who have influenced me and impacted my journey that, if I named them all, I'd have to start a whole new book. But here are some of the shining stars in my life who absolutely need a major shout out:

Tots obvs, my mother, Meredith Rabino. Everything I've learned about badassery is from this woman.

My hubby, Dusty Bernal, who supports, encourages and loves me despite, and because, of all my shenanigans.

My ride-or-dies, my OG running partners, and my BBF BFFs Genevieve Bilanzich Stearns and Tamra Harris. There are no two humans who can blow up my Marco Polo quite like y'all. I love you two to the moon and back.

Kym & Pete Buttschardt, who create ripple effects every day that become massively impactful for so many people. Thank you for seeing something in me I didn't see for myself. Because of you, I have been changed for good.

Bryan Palmer, for being the first person to tell me I should write a book. You planted a seed that day and look what grew from it.

To the amazing team that helped get this Cinderella ready for her Book Cover Ball: Myke Huncharek Dy, the most amazing hair and makeup artist; Bayley Goldsberry, photographer extraordinaire; Sara Mejeur, gangster Sharpie tattoo artist; and Clairesse Miljour, dear friend and moral support provider.

Meghan Stevenson and Christy Stevenson (no relation to each other, although the latter is my sister), for providing me editorial advice, suggestions, and pointers; for being the second and third set of eyes on my manuscript, and not judging me too harshly.

To tribes loved and lost. Thank you for coming into my life at exactly the right moment to help me along on the part of my journey you were meant to be on. And thank you for the valuable life lessons I learned when your time on my journey expired and we went our separate ways.

A slew of badass women who have helped lift me up in one way or another:

Jody Baird, Amanda Schleininger, Jessica Adams, Sage Rabino, Shelby Palmer, Harmony Nordgren, Molly Bitton, Devi Cooper, Nina Rizer, Amy Hanges, Rikki Wright, Mandi Nilson, Jacqui Ball, Adrienne Andrews, Shauna Ray, Hollie Godfrey, Jodi Orgill Brown, Crystalee Webb Beck, Shayla Chavez, Kelli Bilderback, Donna Miner, Shannon Olsen, Haley Soto, Becky Gutierrez Espinoza, Jaynee Nadolski, Abby Monroe, Rizza Rabino, Danielle Croyle, Hollie Dance, Carrie Butler, Sarah Schelin, Cindy Weloth, Aundrea DeMille, Russie Edwards, Cindy Bernal, Portia Yokel, Carla Williams, Dena Jansen, Jennifer Hashimoto, Marianne Bernal, Kathy Buller, LaVonne Sandberg, Crystal Guillen-Fortugno, Mel Miller, Priya Nembhard, Ashley Wolthuis, Deni Mooney, Rikki White, Pat Thomson, Kaelee Miller, Roberta Dustin, Kim Thomas, Tracy Valdez, Kristen Floyd, Jill Charnews, Heidi Flitton, Kimberli Green, Brittney Chugg, Elizabeth Hill, Emily Vause, Carrie Lindsay, Heidi Benson, Josepha Woolever, Tiffani Shisler, Mari Roberts; and Jena Flowers, Katie Barton, Stacey Miller and Kellie Kezior for being there on one of the hardest days of my life.

And to you, dear reader, for letting me share my story with you.

THE BEGINNING

"You see the smile that's on my mouth
It's hiding the words that don't come out
And all of my friends who think that I'm blessed
They don't know my head is a mess
No, they don't know who I really am
And they don't know what
I've been through like you do
And I was made for you

And all of these lines across my face
Tell you the story of who I am
So many stories of where I've been
And how I got to where I am
But these stories don't mean anything
When you've got no one to tell them to
It's true, I was made for you
It's true that I was made for you."

--Brandi Carlile, "The Story"

I once had this genius idea to start a business of upcycling glass bottles into wind chimes, vases, and whatever other whimsical things struck my fancy. I was a bartender at the time, so I had access to plenty of materials for my brilliant plan. I bought a fancy little contraption online that simplified the process of cutting the glass bottles and I got to work on my projects. I assembled one windchime using a Grey Goose bottle with a martini glass hanging out of the bottom. I made another one out of a wine bottle, using a wine key as the hook and hanging a wine glass from the bottom. I was pretty proud of my clever creations. And I was getting really good with the bottle cutter, so much so that I decided to ditch the cumbersome protective gloves I should have been wearing.

One Sunday morning, still dressed in my thin night gown, I leisurely sipped coffee in the kitchen while listening to a chill station on my Pandora app. I had a bunch of bottles on the counter from my shift the night before that were on my list for that day's transformations. My two boys were playing in their rooms and my husband was in our bedroom getting ready for work. I set my coffee mug on the counter and picked up an empty Bud Light bottle, singing softly to the music that wafted from my phone. While the liquor and wine bottles were great for bigger projects, I had plans to use the smaller beer bottles to create votive holders. I attached the glass cutter to the bottle and started to turn it around the bottle's circumference.

Liquor and wine bottles are substantially thicker than beer bottles and therefore can handle the pressure of a glass cutter being clamped on and twisted around them. I had already done dozens without incident. Beer bottles, I was about to realize, being much thinner, don't hold up very well under the same pressure. As I held the base of the bottle with my left hand and turned the bottle cutter with my right hand, the bottle shattered and my right hand slipped down the jagged crack.

I knew immediately the cut was deep. I leaned over the sink and turned the water on, watching as a steady flow of bright red blood swirled down the drain. I grabbed a dish towel off the refrigerator door and wrapped it around my pinky so I could examine the damage. Through the stream of blood, I caught a glimpse of white that I figured was either bone or tendon. I felt lightheaded and heard a high-pitched ringing in my ears. Afraid I might pass out, I gripped the counter and called out to my husband who was two rooms away.

"Babe," I said in a quavering voice. "Babe, I need you."

Somewhat impatiently he replied, "What? What do you need?"

"Just come here please. I cut myself and it's pretty bad."

He came into the kitchen and assessed the situation, looking at the shattered bottle on the counter then to me, queasily leaning over the sink.

"Oh my gosh. Did you do that cutting a bottle?"

I nodded sheepishly. He took a quick look at my finger which, by now, had soaked through the kitchen towel. Not one for guts and gore he said, "You should probably ask your mom what to do."

My mom was a nurse and therefore the family medical professional for any and all bumps, bruises, rashes, coughs, cuts, and other ailments and illnesses. I texted her a picture of my wound with the message, "What do you think?"

She called me almost immediately.

"Is that YOUR finger? What did you do? I told you you were going to hurt yourself, cutting those damn bottles."

"Do you think I need stitches?" I sniffled.

"Um, yeah, I do."

Shit, I thought. "Dusty has to go to work. Can you meet me at the InstaCare?"

I wrapped a fresh towel around my pinky and changed into some sweats and a hoodie. My husband called his dad to come over and stay with the boys and then he dropped me off to the clinic on his way to work. I apologized for what felt like such a stupid mistake on my part. If only I had been wearing gloves. He said not to worry and to text him with an update, but I sensed that he was put out and thought I could have just put a Band-Aid on it. My mom, coming to my rescue as she had so many other times in my life, was already at the clinic waiting for me. She took another look at my pinky, shook her head and confirmed that it was a damn good cut. I was almost proud that I managed to impress my nurse mom with the depth of my gash.

We were the first people there that Sunday morning so we got in with the on-call doctor right away. He was a nice, dark-haired, fit guy in his early forties. When he asked what I had been doing to cause the injury, my mom rolled her eyes and explained that I was trying to make stuff out of bottles.   "You should just stick to drinking it, Stacy. Were you drinking when you did this?" My mom, the comedienne.

The doctor, whose badge read "Lance Capener, M.D.", chuckled and assured me he'd get me all fixed up. He examined my gnarled pinky and confirmed that the white I had seen was indeed my bone. Again, I couldn't help but feel an odd sense of pride for having inflicted such pain on myself. As he stitched my finger back together— two internal stitches and ten external—we made small talk.

Somehow we got on the topic of fitness and I learned that he was a fellow marathoner as well as a triathlete. I told him triathlons were on my bucket list and he encouraged me to do it. He finished with the stitches, bandaged up my now Franken-pinky, and sent me on my way. I texted Dusty to boast about my twelve stitches.

I never cut another bottle after that. When I went to work the next day and my co-workers asked me what the hell had happened, I was embarrassed to admit my grand ideas of glass upcycling were crushed, much like the Bud Light bottle. I carried trays right-handed and I couldn't even do that with my mangled finger. I felt like a dismal failure. I packed up all the bottles I had been collecting along with the glass cutter and gave them away to someone braver, and hopefully smarter, than me.

I had never realized how much I used or how important my pinky was. At the gym, I struggled lifting weights, unable to bend my little finger around free weights or barbells. I tried doing a Body Combat class and realized I couldn't make a fist. Push-ups pained me when I tried to splay my hand out, and there was no way I could have put pressure on it. And making a pinky promise? Out of the question. But eventually, as wounds tend to do, the pain lessened, the stitches were removed, and the once open flesh became a small, shiny scar that wound around my finger.

A little over a year later, on a sunny day at the beginning of June, Dr. Lance Capener took his wife, his daughters and a couple of their daughters' friends boating to celebrate the end of the school year and the start of their summer shenanigans. On the lake, a sudden windstorm swept in, creating six- to ten-foot waves, which caused their small boat to capsize. Dr. Capener's wife and two of his daughters' fourteen-year-old girlfriends were found by rescuers and survived the accident. Lance, his two daughters ages seven and fourteen, and another fourteen-year-old friend died that day, most likely due to hypothermia. Everyone had been wearing a life vest. The county sheriff told news reporters it was the single worst tragedy he had seen on the lake in his more than twenty-nine years with the department. In one very fleeting moment, the Capener family of five was reduced to a widow and her son.

When I read this story in the newspaper the next day, a picture of the entire Capener family printed above the article, smiling from what looked like a beach in Hawaii, I wept. I wept for the woman who lost her two daughters and husband; for the other family who lost their daughter; for the families whose daughters survived such a harrowing experience; for the son who lost his dad and sisters; for the search and rescue team; and for the community impacted by such a sad and devastating loss.

I had only shared the one brief moment in Dr. Capener's care, but I knew he was a good guy. That short time with him created a memory for me that would last my lifetime. The scar on my finger, along with the tingle of permanent nerve damage, reminds me every day of the fragility of life, the power of connection we share to one another, and how moments create ripples that make up the stories of who we become.

When I did my first triathlon in 2016, I thought back to the conversation we had had while he distracted me with small talk and deftly stitched my finger back together. At the time, completing a triathlon was a very distant idea that maybe I would or would not ever do. But he encouraged me that day and helped plant the seed of an idea that would eventually grow into a reality. He became a small part of my story.

In our lifetimes, our paths will cross, intersect, overlap and parallel with countless others' paths. So many stories with varying perspectives of each of the storytellers. In 2017, I met a guy through my running group who was a cool, quirky dude, known for his penchant of playing dress-up when he ran. He once posted a few pictures in our Facebook group of some of his top running costumes: a wedding dress complete with a veil, a caveman getup, and a Playboy bunny bow tie and black Speedo, to name just a few.

I laughed when I saw them and couldn't help feeling like I had seen the Speedo somewhere before. I started scouring old race pictures and lo and behold, I found a picture of my friend Quennie from the 2010 Las Vegas Ragnar, a twelve-person relay race. In the background I spotted a familiar half-naked, Speedo-clad body.

Quennie, who had been my arch nemesis in high school in South Carolina after she started dating my ex-boyfriend Bobby, had reached out to me a few years earlier via myspace. (myspace, for those who don't know, was the largest social networking site from 2005 to 2009.) She apologized for how mean she had been in high school and we connected over our shared love of running. She lived in California and I was in Utah, so when I had some friends who wanted to do Vegas Ragnar, she excitedly joined us.

Quennie was a couple years older than me and was intimidating as hell. My sophomore year, we ended up in the same French class with Monsieur Lloyd, who was also the school's tennis coach and the object of many a girl's (and probably some boys') crush. Twice during the school year, we had to prepare a traditional French dish for the class. Both times, Quennie's dishes were culinary masterpieces. Mine were what would today be described as "Pinterest Fails."

Quennie also had amazing long, black hair. Later, when we started doing races together, we marveled at her ability to twist her hair into messy, sweaty buns which she would later unravel into perfectly waved tresses like a damn Herbal Essence commercial.

When I made the connection that a guy I had met in 2017 was a random stranger in Quennie's picture from seven years prior, my mind was blown. I wondered how many other times our paths had likely crossed over the years, probably at a race. I thought about how many other people's paths I had intersected with throughout my life. What stories was I a part of? In whose pictures was I the random stranger in the background? How was my perspective of the story different from someone else's?

I kind of always knew I was the product of my life's experiences, good and bad. And I think a part of me felt like the only stories worth sharing were the good ones, the victories, the accomplishments. The rest of the stories, the ones people don't generally like to talk about, were best swept under the rug. And so, for many years, that's exactly what I did. The parts of me that were less than perfect were silently shelved away, occasionally opened and shared, but only with a select few and usually under some oath of secrecy from them. I only ever wanted people to see all that was good and right in my world. Until eventually, little by little, that charade became so damn exhausting. I think as I got older, the idea of trying to be one thing for someone and another thing for somebody else—I simply lacked the energy to do it.

In my late thirties and early forties, I decided to start truly owning my story. And wow; how liberating, exciting, terrifying, joyous, and sorrowful my journey became. I gained respect and admiration from some people, and I lost friendships with others. I was the same person all along but shifting my perspective and sharing my story altered friendship dynamics in ways I couldn't have foreseen. The lines across my face, the stretch marks across my body, the tattoos inked into my skin, and the scars created from life's mishaps and mistakes—those tell my stories. And, like most everyone else I've met on this giant rock floating through space, I have some damn good stories.

In my lifetime, I have played the victim role in some of my stories: childhood sexual abuse, teenage birth mom, three-time divorced single mom, autism mom. And sometimes, I have assumed the role of the villain. I have lied, cheated and stolen; I have driven home from bars on nights when I definitely shouldn't have. I have lashed out, sometimes bold-faced, sometimes passively-aggressively, at people I loved. That's a hard fact to acknowledge, knowing that in someone else's story, the character I played wasn't so nice.

I am definitely not without my fair share of guilt for screwups. I hate knowing that I have hurt people in my wake. I also know I probably won't ever be able to run for any sort of political office since I have a lot of skeletons lurking in my closet. But like a phoenix in Greek mythology that cyclically regenerates, I have been reborn from the ashes and, I like to think, become a better, nicer badass in the process.

I've learned that the hard times are what build our character and make us who we are. I am grateful for the bad parts; I am thankful for the paths I crossed with people who broke my heart and my spirit. Those experiences built me up after tearing me down. I survived days and nights when I legitimately thought I was going (and even wanted) to die. I hit a rock bottom, pretty hard, and while I lingered there a little longer than I maybe should have, I only stayed there long enough to realize I didn't want to stay there.

I once went to a presentation where the speaker said, "You can pass through hell but you don't need to build a house there." Amen, sister! Preach! I hated who I was during that time, walking alone through my personal hell. I was completely disconnected from myself; I felt like a shitty mom; I loathed the reflection of the woman staring back at me in the mirror. I was disgusted with who I had become and I felt hopeless about any chance of redemption. Through the darkness though, I found a glimmer of light. I had a small sliver of hope that there was more, that I was capable of greatness, and that there was no way to go but up. As Oscar Wilde wrote, "We are all in the gutter, but some of us are looking at stars."

Since 2008, I've spent over ten years in a sort of metamorphosis. I have done impossible things. I actually like who I am now (as long as I don't fall down any Instagram rabbit holes of picture-perfect celebs and influencers). I thought I could only achieve this level of self-love if I *never* admitted to my transgressions from my previous life; never talked about being abused or giving a son up for adoption.

I was shamed into silence for years, directly and indirectly. All the parts of myself that I was so worried about what people would think became the very bits that made me proud, even somewhat extraordinary. Opening up and sharing my story, while incredibly terrifying and making me feel extremely vulnerable, has been the most empowering change I could have made in my life. As my homegirl Brené Brown wrote in *The Gifts of Imperfection* on the power of connecting through story:

"…courage has a ripple effect. Every time we choose courage, we make everyone around us a little better and the world a little braver. And our world could stand to be a little kinder and braver."

See? While sharing my story scares the ever-living shit out of me, the courage I've mustered to do so makes others (possibly even YOU) a little better and a little braver. You're welcome. Oh, and full disclosure: Brené isn't my homegirl…yet. But she's on my list. Along with Michelle Obama, Ellen, Oprah, and Pink. Hear that ladies?? I'm coming for you! (Not in a creepy stalker way. In an "I wrote a book and mentioned you in it, so can we be friends now?" sort of way.)

My mantra for 2018 was "Voice." Finding the courage to speak up about the stuff people don't want to talk about. Advocating for and building awareness of struggles of raising an autistic son. Fighting against childhood abuse. Bravely sharing my adoption story. The more I have shared my voice, the more others have accepted the invitation to share theirs. In a way, I have helped pave the way for people to find the courage to open up about their own hardships.

Because **we are not alone**. We are human, we make mistakes, we do dumb shit. It doesn't mean we are bad people beyond redemption. There is always hope. We just have to bring what has been kept in the darkness to light and know that there are those who will love us despite, and because of, our flaws.

I know many other people have experienced their own unique, quirky, crazy life turns that led to their own sort of existential crisis. Because really, all we are is the culmination of every experience we have ever had—good, bad, ugly, beautiful. We are made up of stories and connect to others through those stories. My journey has been made possible by so many others who came before me, sharing their stories, inviting me to share my own, and intertwining our stories together to create a tapestry of possibilities.

Part of my purpose, as I've recently discovered, is to speak my truth, share my stories, and leave my mark on the world. Somehow, my stories are meant to help others on their own journeys, just as my life has been impacted by those before me. Some of my stories are pure magic, lovely and inspiring. Others are borne from places of darkness. I honor all of them for the role they played in building me into the woman I am today. I hope they find those who can benefit from hearing them.

A couple of years ago, I joined my local chapter of the National Speakers Association, where I learned some valuable information as a new, eager, up-and-coming speaker. One of the uber successful guest speakers once said two things that caused some major cognitive dissonance for me: "Be authentic onstage" and "You should never swear onstage."

If you've made it to this point in the book, you can probably imagine why my brain couldn't connect these two obviously conflicting thoughts. I am a pretty authentic person (I once took an online character assessment that rated honesty as my number one quality and y'all know the internet is never wrong). I am also a swearer. In my defense, I am the byproduct of a nurse and a sailor, so swearing is practically in my DNA. I mean, don't get me wrong— I'm no Gary V. I don't superfluously drop F-bombs. But when the occasion calls for it, I've been known to use some PG-13-language.

Another gem I took from an NSA meeting is that no matter who you are, how great your message is, or how awesome everyone else thinks you are, there will always be people in the audience who do not connect or engage with you. It more than likely has very little to do with you and everything to do with them. I have found this to be pretty accurate, even though most of the feedback I've gotten has been positive. I can even usually tell, depending on the size of the group, who the haters are. (Although sometimes I've seen some major Resting Bitch Face, only to have them come up to me afterward, gushing about how much they enjoyed my presentation. Goes to show you can't always trust RBF.)

I know I am not everyone's cup of tea— and I don't claim to be nor do I want to be. I recently received a rejection email from a meeting planner who wouldn't hire me due to the "bad language" in my "come-on." Because I call myself an Ambassador of Badassery, meaning: "I see the Badass in YOU and I help you see it, too." Shortly after receiving that rejection, I was hired for an event where they were thrilled to have a "kickass" speaker—and it was my highest paid gig at that point. Those are my people! Some speakers are Pollyanna and some speakers are Pink. I'm a Pink kind of girl, myself. #obvs

I hope that if you are reading this book, if you are taking the time out of your busy life to consume these words, you are doing it with an open heart and mind. I *really* hope you're reading this book of your own free accord and that you didn't get suckered into it by your book club or it was recommended to you by someone who clearly has no idea in your taste. If that's the case, you should probably dump that book club and/or friend immediately if not sooner. But I hope you'll still read this book. I really think there are some gems here.

I regularly attend my local chamber's women in business networking events and recently we discussed Rachel Hollis's book *Girl, Wash Your Face.* The room buzzed with positive energy as the women shared their favorite parts of the book. The conversation was upbeat until an older woman chimed in, "I don't get it. I don't know what all the fuss is about. I hated it." (Sorry, Rachel.) All the other women awkwardly looked around at one another, not sure how to proceed with the discussion. Experiences like this make me really worried about putting myself out there, knowing there will always, *always* be people who don't like you.

I address some heavy topics here, hopefully in an enlightening and entertaining way. But, like life, some of the stories are hard. I hope that if I share something that you don't like that you will give me some grace. If I "trigger" you, which I've been told before that I've done, I hope you take the time to reflect and figure out what work you might need to do. As Licensed Marriage and Family Therapist Vienna Pharaon said, "Avoiding your triggers isn't healing. Healing happens when you're triggered and you're able to move through the pain, the pattern, and the story, and walk your way to a different ending."

I avoided my triggers for more than two decades. Y'all, I do not, I repeat, do NOT recommend doing that. Moving through the pain, the pattern, and the story has brought me so much joy, and not only did I walk my way to a different ending, I ran to it. I continue to run to it today. I hope this book inspires you to do the same.

There's a quote I heard recently at a retreat for mama entrepreneurs (#mamaspringbreak) that said: "The shortest distance between two people is a story." If the shortest distance between two people is a story, well dear reader, we are about to become best friends forever #BFF. (We should probably schedule a session to get matching tattoos.)

I once did a presentation and afterward received this feedback: "She shared her story and her obstacles, but she didn't tell us how to overcome ours."

For the record, I had an entire slide titled "Bullets to Badassery" with a list of ways to work on one's own inner badass. But alas, her perspective was her reality, and she didn't take away what I had hoped to share with her. Here's the catch, and what I want you to realize: Sometimes the lessons you need to learn aren't going to be in How-To DIY form. There is no manual, no step-by-step checklist on how to best live *your* life. Some of the greatest lessons you learn are going to be from the telling of the story itself.

I've gone to a zillion seminars and heard a ton of speakers share tips, tricks, tactics and life hacks. I've read hundreds of self-help, personal development, and spiritual growth books. You know what my biggest takeaway was from all of these? Stories. Learning about the amazing accomplishments all these humans achieved. That's where the inspiration comes from. Because seeing what others have done means maybe, just maybe, I can do something awesome too.

This is not a Self-Help book, I am no Life Coach, there are no hard and fast rules here. These are stories meant to connect with those who need them. I'm excited for our journeys to intersect. I'm happy you've chosen me to become part of your story. I hope you enjoy some of mine, in all their messy, funny, ugly, heartwarming glory. I can't wait for you to share yours, too.

CHAPTER ONE:
FOREVER A FAILURE

"Think like a queen. A queen is not afraid to fail. Failure is another stepping stone to greatness." ~Oprah Winfrey

Three and a half miles. That is the distance from my house in a quaint neighborhood, perched on a small hill, to the local Department of Workforce Services. Just over three miles, close proximity, the distance of an easy run. I know because I mapped it the other day after driving by on my way to a trendy, new, much talked about vegan coffee shop in a previously blighted area of town that had been and continues to be revitalized. When I passed the drab two-story brick building, I uttered a barely perceptible, "Oh yeah." It had been about ten years since I had been to the DWS, years that felt like a lifetime ago. Enough time that I had almost completely forgotten about the months I had spent in and out of that building, filling out paperwork, taking mandatory classes, awaiting my monthly benefits so that I could afford to get groceries for my son Haiden and myself.

When I wound up in that situation at thirty-one-years-old, it wasn't the first time I had been there and, I figured, it wouldn't be the last. When I had my daughter as a single mom at nineteen, I was on Medicaid and food stamps. I was what some refer to as a "burden to society," someone who "worked the system." I was working and going to school but was broke and uninsured. I hated that I was a societal leech, depending heavily on help from others. I spent years of my adult life trying to break out of the cycle and it seemed like I would never make it. Multiple divorces, employment instability, and eventually filing a bankruptcy, I accepted my role of failure and played the part magnificently. I was a perpetual victim of my circumstances and I felt like I deserved it when bad things happened to me. And then, when I ran my first marathon, everything, and I mean *everything,* changed.

Here is what I knew when I trained for and ran my first marathon in 2009: It was hard. It was time-consuming. It hurt. It was stinky. It took dedication and discipline. Each week I had to increase my mileage, I knew there was no way in hell I would be able to run that many miles. And yet as the weeks progressed, so did my ability to log the incrementally increasing distances.

Here is what I *didn't* know when I trained for and crossed the finish line of my first marathon: I was building character, creating a more badass version of myself than I could have ever imagined. Only about one percent of the population will ever run a marathon. Running a marathon kind of made me special. I had no idea! Putting 26.2 miles between who I was at the starting line when the gun went off and who I was just over five hours later when I crossed the finish line was a total game-changer. Joining the ranks of the one percent changed my life's trajectory. If I was a finisher then that meant maybe I was no longer a failure.

To test this hypothesis, I decided in the fall of that same year that I would sign up for classes in the spring at the local college, Weber State University. I was waiting tables, had no money, no reliable daycare for my then four-year-old son Haiden who, by the way, had recently been diagnosed with autism, AND it was my fourth attempt at going to college. When I proudly announced my decision to my family at Thanksgiving my mom, in her nicest mom voice, said, "Are you sure you should do that? We all know school isn't your forte." I puffed my chest indignantly and replied, "This time is different. Because now I'm a marathoner. And if I can do that, I can do anything." (Cue empowering theme music.)

She did make a good point though. I definitely had a reputation for starting things, all sorts of gung-ho, only to fizzle out a short time later. My first college attempt had been when I was eighteen and I only lasted one semester. My next college attempt was about a year later. That time around I managed to get two semesters under my belt before I threw in the towel. In my defense, I had given birth to my daughter, so between work, school and juggling single mamahood, dropping out of school was a tremendous relief. Plus, I really had no idea what I wanted to do. I had considered following in my mother's footsteps and going into nursing, but blood and needles gave me the major heebee geebees, so there was no way I could do it. My third attempt, I signed up at a community college to get an associate degree in Hospitality Management. I racked up a shit ton of student loans (using most of the money to live on) before deciding I could work my way into management (I was working at Olive

Garden) without actually having a degree.

When I registered for classes at WSU for the Spring 2010 semester, my internal flame burned strong and bright. Still, there was a nagging voice in the back of my mind that occasionally popped up to remind me that I did tend to quit things when the going got rough. I worked constantly to keep that annoying voice (think Fran Drescher in "The Nanny") at bay, but man sometimes that bitch was loud. Case in point: the 2010 Ogden Marathon.

I was in my first semester and was working two jobs—one as a marketer for a title and escrow company and another, of course, waiting tables—and single-handedly taking care of Haiden. To say I was stretched thin is an understatement. Training for what would be my third marathon was the thing that unfortunately dropped low on the totem pole of priorities in my life at that time.

The funny thing about marathons is that, for me, they pushed my body to a level of pain I had never before experienced. But, retrospectively thinking, what truly got me to the finish lines was my mental capacity to believe that I could. To picture myself, each arduous mile marker I passed on the course, crossing the finish line and having a medal draped around my sweaty neck. I was convinced that running a marathon was ninety percent mental, ten percent physical. I know—what a stupid theory. And I was about to realize this when I started the race that day in 2010, not knowing the heartbreak it would end in.

I guess I should back up here and explain that the problem didn't start the day of the marathon; it actually started the day before when I decided to do a pre-race shake out five-mile run. And I don't want it to sound like I wasn't prepared or hadn't trained at all for this race. I had. I had gotten in my long runs but my weekly shorter runs left something to be desired. Why I decided to run those five miles the day before the marathon, I don't know. But when I did, I ended up getting a blister on the fourth toe of my left foot. No problem, I thought. I'll just wrap it up with some moleskin.

There is a mantra among runners: Don't try anything new on race day that you've never tried in training. That goes for shoes, socks, your clothing, your nutrition, your technology, everything. If you haven't taken it for a trial run (haha, see what I did there?) race day is NOT the day to do so. I had never before used moleskin on a blister, so trying it the day of a marathon was my first mistake. I had wrapped it around my blistered toe and hoped for the best as I set off on my run. I could feel it rubbing incessantly between my toes the entire time. By mile five, it had become so uncomfortable that I stopped and took it off altogether but at this point it was too late—I had created another blister.

I was in pain but I felt like it was somewhat manageable. What had started as a small blister on the underside of my toe the day before was now a mega blister that wrapped from the inside of my toe to the underside. I could feel it pulsing and pounding with every step I took. At mile sixteen, the road that ran alongside Pineview Reservoir before the course dropped runners into Ogden Canyon, I felt a gush of warmth in my sock as the blister popped. I hobbled over to an aid station and assessed the damage. Blood stained my sock and my toe looked pretty mangled. A kind volunteer bandaged my toe and gave me Ibuprofen. I was disappointed that the whole debacle was slowing down my goal pace but figured now that the blister had popped, I would be able to get back on track.

*Side note: Do y'all know that celebrities like Will Ferrell, Alicia Keys, Al Roker, and Oprah Winfrey are all marathoners? Oprah ran the Marine Corps Marathon in 1994 in four hours and twenty-nine minutes. I have run multiple marathons telling myself, "Beat Oprah, beat Oprah." (Sorry, Oprah.) I have yet to beat Oprah. Or Will Ferrell's best time for that matter. He ran a 3:56 in 2003! Dude was fast. I have, however, beat Alicia's and Al's times. But enough about that. Let's get back to the story.

As I headed toward the mouth of the canyon, I quickly realized that the pain wasn't any better and, in fact, felt even more excruciating. In an effort to avoid putting pressure on my left foot, I started overcompensating with my right. It didn't take long for my body to tell me that was a big hell no, as jolts of pain shot through my right hip. I limp-hobbled to the next aid station which was just over the eighteen-mile mark. I sat delirious in a chair while another kind woman took a look at my foot. She said there wasn't much more that could be done that we hadn't already tried and that continuing the race could cause more damage. I blinked at her and asked, "And I'm eight miles from the finish line?" She nodded sympathetically. I tried to picture myself, carrying my broken body for eight. more. miles. So close, so far away. I thought of how much pain I had been in to get me to where I was currently sitting, surrounded by cheerful volunteers who handed out orange slices and halved bananas to the runners. And then the woman told me, "There will always be another race. Today is not your day."

Tears mixed with my sweat and coursed down my face. I nodded, accepting my defeat. Fran Drescher's voice creeped into my brain, taunting my failure. The aid station volunteer helped me over to the bus that was meant for the relay runners who would be shuttled to the finish line after their six-mile segment of the marathon. There was a happy buzz among the crowd as I sunk down into a seat, trying to hide my ugly-crying. A woman next to me asked me if I was okay and, after I explained what had happened, offered me comforting words. (The next year, at a Ragnar Relay race, I would run into her again and feelings of embarrassment would wash over me when she recognized me. Note to self: Don't leave witnesses to your failures.)

I couldn't believe it. I couldn't help the feelings of bitter disappointment and utter heartbreak that I was "DNF-ing" a race. DNF = Did Not Finish. The Scarlet Letters of the running world. I thought after running my first marathon that I had left my days of failure behind me. Now, it sat heavily with me as I rode the yellow school bus through the canyon toward the finish line, sobbing defeatedly. I was not invincible and any contrary notion was idiotic.

I decided to back off a little from running, accepting that I didn't have the time to put into marathon training while also going to school full-time. But when registration opened for the 2011 Ogden Marathon, like a dumbass moth to a big ass flame, I signed up again. I was consumed by the need for redemption. I trained as much and as well as I could, fighting a knee injury that almost sidelined me and mountains of homework. At one point I strongly considered selling my race entry and dropping out. But the fighter in me couldn't do it. On race day, I gave it everything I had. A couple miles from the finish line and multiple blisters on my feet, I took off my shoes and ran/limped the remainder of the race in my socks. There were hardly any spectators left and the race crew had started dismantling the finish line as I hobbled my way through the chute. It was ugly but I did it.

And I was back! Or so I thought. I would eventually run more marathons and I'd experience more injuries and setbacks. Each time I got knocked down, I got back up. I convinced myself I no longer identified as a failure so my only option was to succeed, as if success begets success in perpetuity. It was unrealistic thinking. But what I learned through the process of getting repeatedly knocked down was that each time I got back up, I was more determined than before. Failing fueled my fire.

One semester, I took a Public Relations course where each student had to submit a campaign proposal for a nonprofit in Salt Lake City. It was a competition open to all the universities in Utah. I jumped all in and was ecstatic when my pitch was chosen as one of the top five from hundreds of submissions. Each of us would have the opportunity to present our ideas to the nonprofit a few weeks later and one of us would earn the title of "Utah PR Student of the Year." I drove home from my class that evening, rocking out to Christina Aguilera, as tears streamed down my face. I couldn't explain why I was so overcome with emotions, except that it felt like a sort of validation. I felt seen. I felt recognized. I felt important. I allowed myself to think of the possibility of winning the competition. Me! Former Mayor of Loserville. For the moment, I didn't feel like a worthless gutter creature. I felt like I had something valuable to say, ideas that were worth sharing and people who were actually listening.

The competition fell on the same day as a half marathon I had been planning on running with one of my best friends Gigi, but she understood when I had to bail on her. (It ended up working out really well, because that same week I found out I was pregnant with my youngest son.) I spent the morning with my competitors, each of us pitching our proposals to the nonprofit board members. I felt really confident with my presentation. A couple weeks later, they announced the winner, and I had placed third.

Now I know what you're thinking: 'Aw, poor girl. There she goes failing again.' And, while you're not wrong, I didn't feel that way. Yes, I was disappointed and yes, I felt like the cute, young, blonde girl who won (who was the only other competitor from my school) had copied a couple of my ideas after we had each done a practice in front of our class prior to the competition. But more than that, I was just so damn proud I had even been a contender. I was grateful that, at the age of thirty-four, I had the opportunity to be doing what I was doing.

Oh, and getting pregnant when I was so close to the finish line of finally graduating college? Yeah—I had a knack for getting knocked up at inopportune times (more on that in Chapter Seven). Pre-marathon Stacy would have used that as another excuse for dropping out and not finishing. But not post-marathon Stacy. In fact, my pregnancy with Eli was serendipitously perfect timing. Since 2010, I had been going full-time back-to-back-to-back semesters but having Eli in June of 2012 meant I got a break for a little while, some much-needed downtime. Also, did I mention I bartended my way through college, thus I also bartended my way through my last pregnancy? Can I tell you how sexy I felt? I could carry cocktail trays of drinks without my hands, just resting it on my belly. (Okay, that might be a slight over exaggeration—but in any case, it was not what I'd consider my finest hour, all Maternity Coyote Ugly.)

It was during this time that I experienced a tiny epiphany about people, success, and failure. See, I had this idea that the people in my circle were my cheerleaders, that they would be happy to see me start achieving some success in my life, especially considering what a dismal failure I had been for so long. And while I did have many supporters in my corner, I was shocked to realize there were some who would just as happily have watched me fail again. This is as true now as it was back then.

At the end of every semester, I waited anxiously for professors to post grades. Now remember, y'all: this was my FOURTH attempt at college. I was not in a "Cs get degrees" frame of mind like my hubby had been when he graduated from WSU in 2003. I am half Filipino and in case you've never heard it: An A minus is an Asian F. So I was allllll about the 4.0 GPA. I busted my ass to get good grades. And when I did inevitably earn that shiny 4.0, I would gleefully share the news to all my Facebook "friends." Because OF COURSE they would all be happy for me, too, right?! I naively thought this until one night at work, when one of my co-workers leaned in and whispered to me, "Be careful what you're posting on Facebook. Some people are saying you're getting pretty full of yourself."

Full of myself. A thirty-five-year-old pregnant bartender. Do you know that my age qualified my pregnancy as "geriatric"? Do you know what geriatric means?? It means my eggs were on the cusp of drying out and my zygote ran a higher risk of growing an arm out the side of his head. It means I was an old ass pregnant drink-slinger! I was surrounded by young, beautiful, perky cocktail waitresses while I awkwardly bumbled around, trying not to knock over liquor bottles with my ginormous bump. I wore a belly band that painfully dug into the tops of my thighs, to help alleviate the shooting pains up my back. By two a.m., after a busy eight-hour shift, my ankles would swell to nearly twice their normal size.

I was the furthest thing from being too "full of myself." The only thing I was full of was baby and gas bubbles. I couldn't believe that my excitement about a semester well done would open myself up to judgment and criticism. I felt deeply hurt that so-called friends would rather me stifle my joy, and for what? My earning a good GPA took nothing away from their own greatness, it didn't diminish their own accomplishments, and my sharing it on social media shouldn't have bothered them. Still, it was a valuable lesson to learn: haters gonna hate.

The good news is I finally stopped working a month before I had Eli. I enjoyed that summer off of work and school before heading back to WSU for fall semester. I only had two semesters left; I could practically see the finish line. I'd go to class during the week, then take care of my boys, and then I'd bartend all weekend. I hated the bar scene, the drunk fools I'd see every night. One night, as the security guys were clearing everybody out of the building, I was summoned to the ladies' restroom to help a young woman who had passed out. When I went into the stall, she was slumped next to the toilet, her short dress hoisted up to her waist and her undies around her ankles. I shuddered at the thought of what kind of nasty germs would creep into her buck ass naked vagina from the disgusting bathroom floor. Also, I was a bartender, not a gynecologist, and I was not paid nearly enough to have first row seats to the beaver show. Instances like this fueled me forward as I got closer and closer to college graduation.

And then, after what was quite literally *years,* I did it: I finally became a college graduate. I graduated Summa Cum Laude with a 3.94 GPA (damn you, Philosophy 2200 and Zoology!!) and was named the 2013 Outstanding Graduate of the Year for Public Relations and Advertising. Hearing my name and walking across that stage is still one of the absolute best moments of my life. I was thirty-six years old when I earned my college degree. And then I went on to become a huge badass success at one of Utah's premier PR firms. Except that last sentence, which didn't actually happen. In fact, during my last semester, I took Senior Seminar which was a class that basically prepared us for finding a job post-graduation. I had mini panic attacks in there all the time, wondering how I would find a job that would also allow me to be a mom first. I had worked so hard to earn my degree, and now I worried how the hell I would actually get to use it.

And the reality was, I didn't. Not right away, anyway. I did get to do some PR work for the company I had interned with during my last semester, but only for a couple months until my boss dissolved the company and went to work for the governor. Then I ended up doing exactly what I had spent years trying to get away from: waiting tables and bartending. The money was decent and the hours worked with my mom duties and my now hubby's schedule, but I was highly underwhelmed.

I also got licensed as a mortgage loan officer, which would have been great if I hadn't realized I HATED dealing with other people's money. Two years post-graduation and I felt like I was floundering, still figuring out what I wanted to be when I grew up. Then, quite serendipitously, in October of 2015 I found out about a position as a sales rep for a home warranty company. I had been in and out of the real estate industry since 2006 (oh, did I not mention that? Yeah, I failed at all of those career attempts too). So when the opportunity came to start this new job, I was thrilled.

The position was a great fit for me because I could pretty much set my own schedule. I had a sizeable territory to cover and I learned quickly how to maximize my productivity while also prioritizing my family. I created my schedule so that I could drop off my boys by 8 a.m. and pick them up by 2:30 p.m., hustling my ass off in between those hours. I often had to drive over an hour to get to different areas where I would visit as many real estate offices as I could before heading back home. My days consisted of coffee appointments, lunches, sales presentations, special events, and committee meetings.

When I got home, I'd get the boys snacks, inquire about their days, let them have some screen time, and continue working. There were days I felt like I was running in a hamster wheel, busy as hell but getting nowhere. Except that, month after month, my paychecks steadily increased. I was, as the proverbial saying goes, reaping the fruits of my labor and damn if it wasn't the sweetest fruit ever. By December of 2017, I had made the most money in my working career (and I had been working since I was seventeen, so that's a long time) and I won a huge industry award as Affiliate of the Year. I was on fire.

But a bit of a plot twist occurred earlier in 2017: I discovered a passion for public speaking. I was the lunch sponsor for one of the Realtor boards I served on. Being the sponsor meant my company paid $250 for the opportunity to market to all the lunch attendees. I could either do a five-minute sales pitch and then they'd have a guest speaker, or I could do the full 45-minute presentation but on a different topic than home warranties. At the time I was reading *The Happiness Advantage* by Shawn Achor, so I put together a presentation about that.

A couple weeks before the luncheon, I gathered a group of friends and did a practice run-through, asking for feedback afterward. A few friends gave me lukewarm reviews and one friend suggested I personalize it more. "You have a great story," he said. "Share it." I completely revamped my slides, emailed the organizer of the luncheon and announced the new title of my presentation: "Failure to Finisher". (Which, coincidentally, was the original title of this book if this book hadn't taken over two years to write and therefore totally metamorphosed from its original outline.)

The day of the luncheon came and I was a sweaty-palmed, dry-mouthed, shaky-hands mess. The crowd of about sixty people was full of business associates I had been marketing for almost two years, and I was about to spill some of my deepest, darkest secrets to them. I shared a few of my biggest failures, especially those I had experienced within the real estate industry. At the conclusion of my presentation, I was shocked when many of the audience members embraced me, sharing bits of their own stories with me. Admitting my own vulnerability allowed them to do the same and we became more connected than we otherwise would have. And then something even crazier happened: I got asked to speak at another event. And then another and another. I realized I loved—like experienced a euphoric high—public speaking.

I did a Google search and learned about the National Speakers Association. Holy shit! There were people who spoke professionally *for a living*! I could totally do that too. I attended a meeting at the local chapter in Salt Lake and joined the next month. I hired a website designer, I set up an LLC, I ordered business cards, I built social media pages for my alter ego, I opened a business bank account. I was officially open for business as a speaker and See Stacy Speak LLC was going to be an overnight, international success! Spoiler: I am in my third year of "building" my business and I am not an international success. (Yet.) How long is this building process supposed to take? But I have spoken all over the state of Utah, twice in Texas, and once in Idaho so technically I'm a national speaker. Hooray!

Coming off my high of record-breaking income and winning my award at the end of 2017, I took all that momentum and came to an almost screeching halt by March of 2018. I really thought I could balance everything I had been doing in my sales role with Elevate Home Warranty while simultaneously working on my own business. It became painfully clear to myself (and anyone else who saw my declining sales numbers) that my heart just wasn't in it anymore. My manager sat down with me in April and asked what was going on. I told him straight up that slinging home warranties wasn't my purpose (much to the chagrin of my hubby who, while always supportive, was also somewhat panicked by how much I "trust the universe" in helping me to manifest my dreams).

My manager seemed surprised by my transparency and told me they didn't want to see me leave the company. Since I wasn't booked up with tons of (ahem, *any*) high-paid speaking gigs, I was content to stay on as long as they would have me. Ultimately, we worked out a deal where I transitioned out of the sales role and became a licensed continuing education instructor instead. This was a perfect fit for me since it put me in front of audiences on a semi-regular basis, giving me lots of practice speaking. Still though, teaching Realtors about home warranties wasn't exactly lighting the fire of my life's purpose.

And that's where I am now: On the cusp of falling backward into the pits of failure once again or taking flight up and away into my greatest success. In 2018, I earned fifty percent less than I had the year prior. Ouch. So far, my 2019 isn't looking much better. My financially responsible hubby only occasionally remarks about the state of affairs of our bank accounts, but I know he's stressing a little. I told him a few years ago that I had a goal of making more money than him. He laughed and asked me why. "Because I want to prove a point. I want to prove that I can." He rolled his eyes and said I was silly and that it wasn't a competition. Maybe not for him, but my Summa Cum Laude ass wants to top his "Cs get degrees" and show him what's up.

It's funny that I run into people who tell me how impressed they are with me but I don't feel impressive. I want to tell them that I feel every day that I should probably start driving for Uber or Door Dash; that most of my speaking gigs are unpaid; that the book I say I'm writing will probably never see the light of day; and that I struggle with Imposter Syndrome all the time. A couple years ago I was nominated to serve on the Board of Directors of my alma mater's Alumni Association. At the first meeting, I felt like a fraud who had no business being there. I had spent so many years as a server that it felt unnatural when the table quite literally turned. I felt like Julia Roberts in *Pretty Woman*, but less like a prostitute. Maybe that's a bad analogy.

The point is, I speak to groups about leadership, empowerment, and finding their Inner Badass, and I struggle to remember my own. Because, while many people see what looks like success and the opportunities I've won, they don't see the pile of rejection emails that is stacked much higher than the yeses. When I'm in my zone in front of an audience, they don't know I'm worried about the balance of my credit card and hoping for a couple good gigs to come through so I can pay it off. I battle anxiety and overwhelm and yet I continue to push forward because I feel a very real sense of making up for lost time. All my years of failure have led to this, and now is my chance to make my mark.

But here is the boldface truth of the matter: The Fran Drescher voice in my head reminds me on occasion that this house I currently enjoy, perched on a small hill with a wall of windows facing eastward toward the majestic mountains and mouth of Ogden Canyon, is a luxury I could never have afforded on my own. The nagging voice knows that, monetarily speaking, I wouldn't be enjoying my current view from the comfort of my vintage green couch were it not for the fact that I married a responsible grownup who pays bills on time, squirrels away money every month into accounts we never touch, and otherwise runs the family finances. Because while I have evolved from the gutter rat I once felt like, I know it's a tightrope I'm on and one misstep will send me falling.

I am a decade and just over three miles from the Department of Workforce Services, far enough away in time but close enough in geographical proximity to remember where I started and why I'm never going back.

CHAPTER TWO:
DEATH OF AN EX

**"There was nothing in the world
That I ever wanted more
Than to feel you deep in my heart
There was nothing in the world
That I ever wanted more
Than to never feel the breaking apart
All my pictures of you."**

~The Cure, "Pictures of You"

I attempted smoking my first cigarette when I was fourteen. My family had gone on a trip to Myrtle Beach, South Carolina, and in one of the souvenir shops I found a gag gift that was a single cigarette encased in a glass tube that read: Break In Case of Emergency. I sneakily purchased it (apparently the cashier didn't require I.D. from me) and smuggled it back to the single-wide trailer where we lived with my mom after my parents' divorce.

I didn't have immediate plans to start smoking, but I had a rebellious inner child who was just waiting to start some shenanigans. The cigarette was tucked away at the bottom of my sock drawer, tempting me daily by its sheer existence. I loved the idea of doing something naughty, just to see what I could get away with. So, one day, when no one else was home, I pulled the novelty gift out of the drawer. I told myself I would tap the glass on the bathroom counter, just to see what would happen. The glass shattered, as it tends to do when smacked on a hard surface, and out fell the cigarette.

I shakily cleaned up the shards of glass and picked up the cigarette. I knew smoking was bad according to our church's policy called "The Word of Wisdom." The document listed all sorts of naughty things to abstain from: coffee, alcohol, tobacco. But holding that slender paper-wrapped stick in my hand, it seemed fairly harmless, like the candy cigarettes my sister and I ate (and pretended to smoke) when we were younger. I went into the kitchen to find a match. I brought it back into my bathroom and plopped down on the carpeted floor. I lit the match with my right hand and touched the flame to the tip of the cigarette that I was holding in my left hand. That's right—I didn't even have the cigarette in my mouth.

I recalled cool movie characters I had seen smoking—Christian Slater and Winona Ryder in *Heathers*— and the light bulb went on in my head. I put the cigarette to my lips, lit it, and took a quick puff that I immediately exhaled. I did that a couple times, watching myself in the mirror. I looked pretty ridiculous, not nearly as cool as Winona, and I didn't particularly care for the taste and smell of it. I flushed it down the toilet, opened the window to air out the smoke, and sprayed some pine-scented Glade. I didn't touch another cigarette... until my freshman year of high school.

I was going steady with a cute but simpleminded surfer dude named Bobby who was a junior. One day after school he was giving me and one of his friends (a cool, artsy girl named Maria) a ride home. As soon as she hopped into the center seat of the truck cab, effectively cutting me off from my boyfriend, she opened up a pack of Marlboro Reds. She offered one to Bobby who took it without hesitation before lighting one for her herself. She turned toward me as if just remembering I was there. "Want one?" she asked.

I didn't, but I sure as hell wasn't going to be shown up by her in front of my boyfriend. I took one, lit it from the glowing coils of the truck's lighter, and turned toward the window to hide the quick puffs and exhales I took. I rolled the window down a few inches as my eyes watered from all the smoke.

After a few months, citing semi-fabricated religious reasons, I broke up with surfer dude Bobby. Shortly after, I started dating a senior. Now, I thought the peer pressure of dating a junior was tough, but I was seriously underprepared to be dating a senior. And he wasn't just *any* senior. He was an extremely popular, well-liked, athletic, philosophical, brooding senior.

The first time I had ever laid eyes on him was the summer of 1988, before my sixth-grade year of middle school. It was a sweltering summer day in Goose Creek and I was riding my bike with my friend Christine, who held onto my shoulders as she stood on the pegs of the back tire. We were riding through her neighborhood, St. James Estates II. My house was in the newer subdivision, St. James Estates III. I never understood why they didn't think of more clever names for these neighborhoods.

As I pedaled down the road, I noticed a group of older boys shooting hoops in a driveway. A tall, tan, lanky boy with wavy sand-colored hair and blue-gray eyes caught my attention. I slowed down and as we coasted by the house, he looked our way and caught me staring.

"Hi," I blurted out.

He flashed me a boyish smile as he lifted his hand in a wave. I felt my face flush and my insides warm up and bubble. Christine, who had an older brother and was privy to such details, leaned into my ear and whispered, "His name is Stacey."

We burst out in laughter, and I began to pick up my pedaling pace, embarrassed and wanting to escape. He would tell me years later he knew that day that I was his soulmate.

The summer before my eighth-grade year was pure hell. My parents were divorcing, and we were selling the house, OUR house, in St. James Estates III. My dad was moving into an apartment in a neighboring city, and my mom, older sister, two younger brothers and I were moving into a single-wide trailer in Birch Hollow, the "nicest trailer park" in Goose Creek. Its walls were plastered with dusty rose-patterned wallpaper and it came complete with matching curtains and comforters. It put the "manufactured" in manufactured home.

To add insult to injury, the move put me in a different school boundary than the one I had been in since fourth grade. As a Navy brat, we had moved every year since kindergarten which meant starting over in a new state, new city, and new school *every* year. We had finally established roots in one place for a few years, only to be unwillingly yanked out. On the first day of eighth grade, I rode the bus with complete strangers, made my way around the hallways with no clue where I was going, and ate lunch by myself. On the bus ride home, a torrential rainstorm pounded the dirt road, turning it to slick, sludgy mud. The bus broke down and I had to trudge home, my new imitation Keds ruined, my Betty Boop earrings ironically, cheerfully hanging from my ears.

When I finally made it home, I flung the trailer door open, threw my soaked backpack inside, and stomped into the living room where my mom sat on the teal-colored couch. For extra dramatic effect, I threw myself to the floor and began to sob. The next day my mom got me a boundary exception to go back to my old middle school. I would ride the bus with my sister to the nearby high school and then walk the quarter mile to my school. At the end of the day, I'd hustle back over to the high school to catch the bus home. All was right with the universe.

One day I was running late leaving my school, so I had to book it to make it to the high school before the bus left. I ran past the football field and the band room, and almost ran into a guy in a black and yellow letter jacket as he strolled through the breezeway. I quickly sidestepped him and glanced back with a hurried, half-assed apology. The words caught in my throat.

Stacey. It was Stacey.

His eyes crinkled at the edges and a spark of recognition lit up his face. He reached toward me, but I had no time to stop. I gestured at my multi-colored Swatch watch, shrugged and continued running toward the bus loading area.

Of *course* St. James Estates II Stacey went to Goose Creek High.

***

Stacey, at six feet three inches, was almost a foot taller than I was. I could see him sauntering down the hall, his head above everyone else's. Our student body population was mostly Black and Filipino, so being a tall Caucasian dude made him noticeable. He wore stone washed jeans and The Doors t-shirts, and he smelled like fresh laundry and Grey Flannel cologne. His back pocket bulged with the telltale circle of a can of Kodiak chew. He was always flanked by other cool jocks, or friends from English class. He was a good ol' southern boy.

I had known who he was for years, remembering him from that summer day. While I dated Bobby the surfer dude, I would see Stacey around school but didn't think much of it. I knew my place, knew he was out of my league, but there was no denying the look in his eyes when I passed by him in the halls. After I broke up with Bobby, when I caught Stacey looking at me, I started looking back. One day, I saw him walking toward me in an otherwise empty hallway. I stopped in front of a vending machine and pretended to be interested in its junky contents. My heart was pounding as I waited for him to pass by. Don't look up, don't look up, don't look up, I told myself.

"Hi," he said casually. I was surprised by his charming southern drawl. It was sweeter and softer than I had imagined.

"Stacy, right?" he asked. I smiled and nodded. He knew damn well who I was and what my name was, but I appreciated his attempt at playing it coy. Months later, in the cafeteria during lunch, friends took immense pleasure in yelling, "STACY!" and then roaring in laughter when we both turned to see who was calling our name. We gained a little bit of high school notoriety as "The Staceys".

I adored him. He would pick me up in his beat up blue Chevette and bring me along to his baseball games, where I would sit alone for hours on end, just for the chance to watch him. I was bored out of my mind, but when he glanced at me on the bleachers, he'd flash his oh-so-cute smile and arch his left eyebrow. He knew I loved that. After the game we'd grab Taco Bell or Burger King or, if we were feeling really fancy, Fazolis where they served never-ending breadsticks doled from the basket of a chipper employee roaming through the restaurant. Then, if we had time, Stacey would shyly ask me if I wanted to go to the golf course. There, parked somewhere in the trees by Hole Six, we'd contort our bodies together, awkwardly, urgently, trying to maneuver over the emergency brake.

I was not his first, nor was he mine; we were each other's "seconds." My V-card had gone unceremoniously to surfer Bobby in his bedroom one day after school. Stacey's had gone to another Filipina during his junior year. She was a naturally beautiful, quiet girl, and for a long time I felt inferior and insecure, knowing Stacey had lost his virginity to her, that he loved Filipinas, and that I was only a "half-breed." When she had broken up with him, he had been devastated. I worried I would never measure up to her. I had no idea, as a naïve freshman in high school, the road that lay ahead for me and Stacey.

He was the first boy who told me, and I honestly believed he meant, that I was prettier than my older sister, Christy. It was always a silly contest between her and me, and a source of contention for years, even within our own family circle. He was the first boy to know why my parents divorced. He knew about my dad's affairs and my sexual abuse. I shared things with him incrementally, gauging his reaction to see when I would scare him off from my messy life. He never wavered. When I was a wreck and life felt like a complete shitstorm, he was the eye of the storm—the calm.

Our favorite pastime was perusing the local Blockbuster store, giggling and flirting as we'd discuss the merits of Keanu Reeves' latest hit. We'd rock/paper/scissor for who got to choose the flick of the night. Then we'd head over to his house, pop some microwave popcorn, slide the VHS into the VCR, and snuggle up uncomfortably in the papasan chair in his room. I'm pretty sure those awkward, saucer-shaped chairs were only meant for one person at a time, but we made the impossible possible.

And, I have a deep, dark confession I've harbored for nearly thirty years: Once, when I left Stacey's house on a rainy, muggy afternoon, I heard the evil buzz of a bloodthirsty mosquito in my car. I reached over to roll down the passenger window to let the sucker out when I heard an ominous thump on the hood of my Isuzu I-Mark. I slammed on the brake and glanced into my rearview mirror. A mailbox post was lying in the yard behind me. Y'all thought I was gonna say 'dog,' didn't you? Well I'm glad it wasn't a dog, but I felt horrible for knocking over someone's mailbox. My brain went to the following places:

1.   My mom was going to kill me.
2.   My sister, with whom I shared the car, was going to kill me.
3.   I had no money to fix the mailbox.

I focused my eyes back toward the road and left the wreckage behind me. I know, I know. I am a rotten person. I'm sure karma has gotten me back for this one. And to the homeowner on Myer Lane who had to right my wrong all those years ago: I am truly sorry. But, hey—at least it wasn't your dog!

After that debacle, I avoided driving over to Stacey's for a little while, and I'd make him do the driving anytime we went anywhere. He'd return me home in time for my nightly curfew and then return an hour or two later as I'd sneak out the back laundry room door of our family's mobile home. The door jamb was tight and would shake the whole trailer if I shut it all the way, so I would grab a bottle of laundry detergent off the washer on my way out and use it to prop the door shut until I returned home. Some nights we'd drive to a secluded spot by the golf course and make-out; other nights we'd drive downtown and walk around Charleston.

One night, after Stacey quietly dropped me off a block away from the trailer, as I approached the back door, my heart skipped a beat and then nearly pounded out of my chest: the bottle of laundry detergent was gone. *Oh shit,* I thought. *Busted.* As I turned the doorknob, I prepared for the shitstorm my mama was about to unleash on me. There, sitting cross-legged on top of the dryer, was my mama. I knew I was in major trouble, but I also felt a calm wash over me that seemed to whisper, "One day you'll look back on this moment and laugh." It took a few years but I'm proud to say we do look back on that moment and get a good chuckle out of it.

My mama tried to keep me from Stacey all the time. She'd ground me, restrict phone calls, and otherwise punish me. I just figured out sneakier ways to see him. (Oh, the gray hairs I must have given her. In a way, my kids are definitely karma for the hell I put her through.) All I knew was that my time with Stacey was quickly running out and I wanted to soak up every last minute I possibly could. Once he left for college, I figured our tryst was trash.

He took me to parties with all his other popular friends which, as a freshman band nerd, made me feel like a bit of a celebrity. It was at one of these parties one night that I truly smoked my first cigarette. Stacey was inside playing a drinking game so I went outside and joined his friend Jeremy on the driveway, seating myself uncomfortably on tiny pebbles.

"You smoke?" he asked. Playing it cool, I nodded and he handed me a Newport. After I lit it, I took a few of my usual quick puffs and exhales. Jeremy looked over at me and chuckled.

"You're not doing it right," he drawled in his lazy southern accent. "You need to inhale." He showed me the technique, sucking in and then exhaling the smoke into little O-shaped rings. It was Christian Slater level cool.

I took a puff, inhaled, and choked. The menthol from the cigarette felt like a blast of winter down my throat and into my lungs. My head started to spin and I had to lie down on the gravelly driveway. Jeremy laughed at me some more.

"Please don't tell Stacey about this," I said, laughing at myself, tears streaming down my cheeks as I continued choking.

Stacey and I dated the rest of his senior year and into the summer after he graduated. I tried to keep my expectations low about the future of our relationship, partly since he'd be leaving soon for college and partly because he warned me that some of his family members were racist and might not take too kindly to his dating me. One Saturday afternoon, he picked me up and we headed for about an hour drive to a town called Santee where they were holding a small family reunion. Very casually, he mentioned, "Don't be surprised if they call you a sand-nigger."

I was mortified. A what? Where was he taking me? I had never been to Santee but I instantly imagined some backwoods, swampy town where lots of gators roamed, ready to gobble up any bodies that happened to get dumped in their vicinity. I pictured his family welcoming us, a group of people in white robes wearing pointed white caps, carrying torches and pitch forks. I begged him to turn around and take me home. He chuckled and said, "No one's gonna really call you that. Not to your face, anyway."

Instances like that solidified my certainty that we were not going to last. As the summer wound down into fall and he was getting ready to leave for Francis Marion University, about two hours from our hometown, I mentally prepared for what I figured was our inevitable breakup. I was getting ready to start my sophomore year at good ol' Goose Creek High (Home of the Gators!) and figured we'd amicably part ways. Then, the night before he left for college, we were at one of the many parties his friends threw when he took me aside, swaying a little from beer buzz, puffing coolly on his cigarette, and leaned into my ear to whisper "I love you" for the first time.

I knew that dropping the L-bomb was monumental, that the last girl he had loved was the one who carried his V-card and had broken his heart. His proclamation of love for me was vulnerable and real, and vocalizing those feelings put a target on his heart at which I might one day take aim. He trusted me with the weight of those words, so what else could I do but reciprocate? I let my guard down and told him I loved him, too.

The next two years of high school, I wore his way-too-big-for-me letter jacket. Our high school colors were black and gold, which actually translated to black and yellow. I resembled a bumblebee who had lost some weight but refused to get a new wardrobe, and I didn't care one bit. Every now and then, when he came home on weekends to visit me, I'd have him spray his cologne inside the jacket so I could wrap myself in his smell when we were apart. If his scent faded sooner than he could get home to refresh it, I'd sidle up to the cologne counter at Dillard's and sneak a couple squirts there. In the halls of GCHS, I carried on his legacy. I was "Stacey's Girl."

**

Smoking in the south was very common and accepted; it was allowed in restaurants, the lobby of the movie theater, and the mall. I never worried about getting my ID checked since I could easily buy packs of smokes from the vending machine at the Waffle House. My smoking habit could be described much like my relationship with Stacey: illogical, on again, off again for years, and toxic. My junior year, we experienced an untimely pregnancy that ended with me graduating a year early, us giving a baby up for adoption, and ultimately a tumultuous, painful breakup with him. A few months after I graduated high school, I moved away from South Carolina and away from him. It never seemed to last long before we boomeranged back to each other.

I had moved to Utah at the end of 1994 to "save my soul" and instead, I got pregnant with my daughter. I moved back home to my mom's house, which by that time was a new place on Bayberry Drive in St. James Estates III. After my parents' divorce, while slumming it in the trailer park, my mom had put herself through nursing school. She was finally back on her feet, just in time to help me get back on mine.

I was a hop, skip, and a jump away from Stacey's parents' house. It was the summer of 1995, and I knew he would be there on break from school. I hadn't seen him in almost ten months, which may as well have been ten years. Late one night, I was listening to the radio when "Satellite" by The Dave Matthews Band came on. Christy, who was also home during summer break from Brigham Young University, turned to look at me. She knew that was one of our songs.

"You're thinking of him, aren't you?"

Tears filled my eyes as I nodded. My heart ached for him so much. We had spoken to each other on the phone a couple times while I was in Utah and he knew I was pregnant and he knew I was coming home. I didn't dare entertain the possibility of getting back together with him, but I also missed him immensely. I took the quick drive to his neighborhood and stood in his parents' driveway, throwing pebbles at his bedroom window. I prayed he was there and I prayed harder that he was alone. The curtains parted, and I saw his beautiful familiar face. I immediately saw it in his eyes that he felt the same way as me. The fact that I was pregnant with someone else's baby was inconsequential. We were impossibly, ridiculously magnetic.

We spent the rest of the summer inseparable. When he went back to school, I signed up for classes at the local community college, mostly to keep myself distracted and busy until my baby came. I also got a job hosting at Outback Steakhouse, where sweet southern patrons would rub my belly, as if they were hoping for a genie to appear to grant them three wishes. I was surprised that strangers touched my baby bump (Bless their hearts!) but also found it oddly endearing. There was no judgment from them, no probing into the drama surrounding my past and this current pregnancy. Just kindness and a sort of adoration.

When I went into labor on a Friday in February 1996, Stacey rushed to the hospital from his college two hours away. I was walking the halls at the Medical University of South Carolina in a hospital gown when I first saw him, and I *blushed*. It was like we were back in the hallway at high school. This boy who knew me more intimately than anyone in the world, who was my soulmate, who had already watched me give birth to a baby, still had the ability to make me blush. When my daughter was delivered, Stacey cut her umbilical cord. I named her Mia (like papaya) Brook— a compromise with Stacey who loved the name Brooklyn. I refused to name my child after a city in New York, so Brook it was.

Shortly after her birth, I moved out of my mom's house and got an apartment of my own. After Stacey graduated college, he moved in with me and Mia. We talked about getting married. There were good days, there were bad days. There were nights he would get blackout drunk. One night after many, many Crown and Cokes, he looked at me and sloppily slurred, "The only reason I want to marry you is so I can be Mia's dad." I went to our bedroom, locked him out, and cried myself to sleep.

Stacey and I struggled to balance our relationship under the circumstances. We were toxic; we were two kids who couldn't logically un-love the other. We loved and we loathed and for a while we made function what was so completely dysfunctional. We argued heatedly and then had make-up sex just as heatedly. I vacillated between wanting nothing to do with him and wanting *everything* to do with him. He was like a nicotine fix. Our relationship was a merry-go-round that I knew would make me sick, but I felt like I could never get off.

On December 15, 1997, Stacey put on a nice pair of slacks, a button-up shirt, and a tie. I put on a tan dress from The Gap. We went to a Justice of the Peace with my mom and Mia and we got hitched. My mom kept Mia for the night so Stacey and I could go to Charleston to celebrate our nuptials. We ate at an Italian restaurant where I ordered a glass of white zinfandel and hoped our cheap Walmart wedding bands made me look twenty-one and I wouldn't get carded.

The next month, I celebrated my twenty-first birthday. My co-workers from Outback wanted to go all out, barhopping all over Charleston, and they did not disappoint. By the end of the night, I was hammered. Stacey was equally, if not more, inebriated than me. We were screaming at each other in a parking lot about how we were getting home. In my drunken haze, I felt the first inkling that we had made a mistake by getting married.

A few months later, having realized his degree in English wasn't getting him too far and he wasn't loving his late-night job of driving a truck and sweeping parking lots, Stacey decided to join the Air Force. When he left for basic training, I was only slightly surprised to realize how liberated, free, and relieved I was by his absence. I decided to leave him, once again, and headed west back to Utah.

***

Despite every effort to put time and distance between us, we continued to boomerang back into each other's lives. We'd split, we'd reunite. Like a nicotine addict, we always came back for more. Over the course of ten years, we flew all over the country to see each other. As the clock ticked down to the possible end of the world during the "Y2K Scare," we celebrated New Year's Eve in New Orleans. We gambled in Las Vegas. I surprised him at the SeaTac airport and we stayed in a Seattle hotel, before he headed to South Korea for a deployment. We partied in Park City. We took a dinner cruise in Biloxi. We explored the salt flats on the way to Wendover. We got loose for my thirty-first birthday in Columbia, SC. We had plans to go to the Grand Canyon, but we never made it there.

In the meantime, I had started running in 2008. I started with a seven-mile race, then a ten-miler, and then my first half marathon.

The race was an hour drive from my home, and to calm my nerves, I smoked a few cigarettes on the way down. The irony wasn't lost on me that I was about to run 13.1 miles as I puffed away on my Marlboro Ultra Lights. In 2009, I ran my first full marathon. I only very occasionally smoked, usually when I drank alcohol. By 2010, I was officially a "former smoker" which felt weird to have to include on annual health checkups. By then, Stacey had taken up space as a "former" in my life as well.

***

In 2013, I married my husband, Dusty. He had been my cheerleader as I put myself through college. He was my rock, my support, my number one fan. We had a son together, and he was helping raise my other two kids. We bought a house, we started our savings, we were building our life. He got the best version of me, when I finally started getting my shit together.

Stacey was a ghost, a "someone I used to know," and certainly not someone I ever spoke of. I had not seen him since 2008 and had not spoken to him since 2009. Yet he was still very much a part of who I was. When my parents had split up and I thought I would die from the pain, he was there. In broken cracks and crevices of my teenage self, such formative years, he had filled those spaces the way the gold epoxy does in *kintsugi* pottery. He was the reason I ordered my steaks medium rare; he was the reason I lost myself whenever I listened to The Cure, The Doors, or Johnny Cash; he was imprinted on my soul.

In the summer of 2016, I heard through the grapevine that he was suffering from effects of many years of prescription drug abuse. As one friend told me in a Facebook message: "He's lost his fucking mind." I felt a distanced sadness, sorry for all the things he was missing out on in life. I also felt a huge amount of guilt: would his life have turned out differently had we stayed together that last time? Could I have saved him from falling off that edge?

A few months later I heard from this same friend that Stacey had been diagnosed with liver cancer, and his prognosis wasn't looking good. I already had a trip scheduled to run a race in North Carolina, so I made some changes to my itinerary so I could go see him. It was October and the east coast was preparing to be hit by Hurricane Matthew. Millions of people were evacuating Charleston, and I was the lone idiot trying to get in. I was terrified, both of being caught in the storm and not making it in time to see Stacey.

When I landed in Charleston, there was an eerie tension in the air—the calm before the storm. I got to my rental car and tuned in to the local radio announcements. The few other passengers on the flight in had warned me that the roads might be shut down and I might not be able to make it downtown to the Medical University. I had come too damn far to not make it now.

There was an apocalyptic vibe as I made my way to the interstate. I nervously checked my rearview mirror, worried I would get pulled over and told to turn the other direction. I drove white-knuckled until I finally made it to the hospital, the same hospital where, more than twenty years prior, Stacey had snipped the umbilical cord to the daughter that wasn't biologically his. If ever there was a time to take up smoking again, that would have been the moment. I was shaking like a leaf as I made my way through the antiseptic-smelling halls. After getting lost, I found the right floor, the right wing, the right room. I was closing the gap between time and distance. I just needed time to stand still for a moment. Stacey was behind the door. I braced myself as I gently knocked and pushed the door open.

***

His sand-colored hair was long and streaked with gray, as was his goatee. His once sparkly blue-gray eyes were sunken, dull and surrounded by dark circles. His usually tan skin was sallow. His boyish features were long gone. He looked tired, sick and full of cancer.

He blinked in shock when he saw me. Even doped up on pain meds, he managed to joke with me in his moments of lucidity. He asked about my husband, asked if he was religious. I told him he was Catholic, and he retorted with: "And he married YOU?" He told the nurses I was his ex-wife and everyone got a good chuckle out of that. After a few hours, when it was time for me to leave, he grabbed my hand and somberly asked, "Did you come here because you think I'm dying?"

"No," I lied, trying to sound cheerful. "I just happened to be in the neighborhood."

He kissed my cheek and told me he loved me. I promised I'd come see him again before I flew home. Unfortunately, Hurricane Matthew wreaked havoc in more ways than I had anticipated. The interstate from Raleigh to Charleston had multiple closures, making it impossible to get back to see him before I flew back home to Utah.

Over the course of the next couple months, Stacey and I chatted and texted a few times. I held out hope that he would fight and win his battle with cancer. By Christmas, he had had a stroke and was unable to communicate. By the first week of the new year, he was on hospice care.

On January 7, 2017, I was sitting in a salon, chopping off ten inches of hair that I was donating to Children with Hair Loss, cancer survivors. Over the years, I had had both long and short hair. I had been planning to cut it for a while— probably as part of my turning-forty-mid-life-crisis—and that Saturday happened to be the earliest one that worked for mine and my hairdresser's schedules. I had known for a few days that Stacey was lying on his death bed, miles away from me. My friend Emily had called to tell me she was going to the hospice center that morning. I sent her a message for Stacey and begged her to read it to him. She told me she would. At 10:10 a.m. she texted: "I just read him your words. Sobbing but I got through. You don't want to see him this way. Trust me. Hold on to your memories from October." At 12:26 p.m. she texted: "He is in heaven."

I read the last message, helpless and broken-hearted. I put my phone in my lap, under the hairdresser's protective cape. I gazed at my reflection. This was the face of someone who had lost a part of their soul. Tears filled my eyes and I fought to keep them from spilling over. I tried distracting myself, fiddling with my phone. Absently, I opened the weather app. My heart skipped a beat when I saw that, despite the odds against such an occurrence, it was twenty-eight degrees where I was and where he was, thousands of miles apart. I had spent many years growing up outside of Charleston and never remember it getting that cold.

When I got home from the hair salon, I went immediately to the closet in the basement where I kept boxes of old memorabilia. Dusty had taken the boys to a movie and I felt a huge relief that none of them would see me in that state of utter despair. Grief, mixed with the overwhelming guilt of *feeling* that grief, painted me into a dark corner of isolation.

I searched, somewhat in a frenzy, for any pictures, mementos, anything that I could touch that was a part of Stacey. Tucked away in an old journal, I found a few letters he had written to me when I had been away for six weeks one summer at Furman University. I cursed myself for having gotten rid of all of our pictures together. In my attempt to move on with life and be a good wife, I had thrown out all evidence of the Stacy/Stacey shenanigans, as if ridding myself of those would rid myself of him completely. We weren't Facebook friends but I scoured through the few pictures I could access on his profile page.

In one of them, he smiled charmingly at the camera, dapper in a bowtie. In another, he sat casually in a chair, tan from a South Carolina summer. I had no idea where these were taken or by whom. In the last photo I found, a lone figure in jeans and a yellow sweatshirt stood, arms outstretched, on beige salt flats, quite a distance from the camera and where the photographer had stood.

It was as if Stacey had left this one picture as a breadcrumb for me, his way of leaving a small trace for me to find my way back to him. Years prior, before drugs took ahold of him, before cancer consumed him, Stacey had pulled off the highway in the middle of nowhere, handed me his camera and instructed me to take his picture. I laughed at him, told him he was stupid. But I watched his back as he walked away from me and when he stopped, raised his face toward the sky, and opened his arms wide, I smiled and snapped the picture.

***

Stacey had never remarried. His obituary listed his school and work accomplishments; he was surrounded by family and friends at the time of his death, and he left behind many friends and fraternity brothers. His "lifelong friend" ex-girlfriend was named, as well as his best friend and his dog. There was no mention that he had ever been married. No sign of a twenty-nine-year history with a girl who shared his same name. It was as if I had never existed in his world.

This reality brought my grief to a whole new level. No one ever tells you how to mourn for an ex. No one tells you how impossible it will feel some days to just keep your shit together, especially in front of your kids and husband. No one wants to hear how your insides feel like you've been shaken upside down and set back down and are expected to stay upright. The few friends you try to confide in seem uncomfortable listening to your heartbreak lament, as if you are making them privy to the details of some scandalous extramarital affair. And you feel it, that *guilt* because you do, in fact, feel so damn broken inside but you're happily married and you hadn't even seen him in so long, so *why* could you possibly be hurting so much?

I'm sure I did a shitty job of mourning him. There was no funeral, no way for me to have closure that way. A casual memorial was planned that May near his birthday, and one of our high school friends added me to the Facebook event. When I made a comment about being unable to make it, his mom took the opportunity to jab at me, saying that I had been a "high school fling" and his ex-girlfriend had been his one true love. It was the saltiest salt in my wound, a wound that many people thought I clearly didn't deserve to feel.

A dead man shouldn't have posed a threat to my marriage, but in the months following his passing, I thought about Stacey more than I had in years. He came to me in dreams and I'd wake up to tears coursing down my cheeks and into my ears. I'd sob silently in the shower, feet from where my husband laid in our bed. I felt racked with guilt, heavy with the secret of how much my heart was broken.

***

Stacey died at age forty-two, exactly three weeks before my fortieth birthday. I had plans to make that year the most epic yet, so I had signed up for a race called the Grand Circle Trailfest. The three-day event consisted of almost forty miles of back-to-back trail runs at Bryce, Zion and the Grand Canyon. It was amazing, majestic, brutal, painful, and beautiful. After the final run at the Grand Canyon, my friends and I headed home, about a six-hour drive.

I was riding shotgun in my friend Kyle's truck, scrolling through Facebook on my phone, when a memory from the previous year popped up and nearly took my breath away. In that moment, I was grateful The Violent Femmes were blaring on the stereo about kissing off into the air, and I was glad I was wearing sunglasses. The hair on the back of my neck prickled, and goosebumps popped up on my arms. Tears streamed down my cheeks and I nearly choked on the lump in my throat.

I hadn't realized when I had signed up for the race the significance of the date. On October 7, 2016, I had been in the hospital room in South Carolina, visiting with Stacey for what would be the last time ever. Exactly one year later and exactly nine months from the day he died, I was running in the Grand Canyon, a place he had always wanted to take me. The son of a bitch finally took me there.

I thought that Stacey's death was one of the most painful experiences I would ever live through. But by the next year, it would be another time of memories and grief that would blindside me so very unexpectedly. Little did I know the full magnitude of the connection I would have to the Grand Canyon.

CHAPTER THREE:
SUICIDE

"Should've stayed, were there signs, I ignored?
Can I help you, not to hurt, anymore?
We saw brilliance, when the world, was asleep
There are things that we can have, but can't keep
If they say
Who cares if one more light goes out?
In a sky of a million stars
It flickers, flickers
Who cares when someone's time runs out?
If a moment is all we are
We're quicker, quicker
Who cares if one more light goes out?
Well I do"
~Linkin Park, "One More Light"

In the late fall of 2009, I hit what I have come to endearingly refer to as my "Rock Bottom." It looked like this:

Three-time divorced woman, mother to a daughter living out-of-state with her dad and stepmom, and a son who had just been diagnosed with autism. I was waiting tables at Applebee's because my "career" in real estate was tanking, along with the relationship/partnership I had built with another Realtor. I had to move out of my boyfriend/business partner's house after discovering he had cheated on me the entire year we were together and I was barely scraping by enough to afford putting a roof over my and my son's head.

I know I said this isn't a self-help book or a list of life hacks, but I do want to leave a few gems here:

- If you ever find yourself checking the web browser history behind your significant other, trust that there's a reason you're having that gut feeling.

- If your S.O. doesn't want to hang up or otherwise display pictures of the two of you together or allow you to stick any type of magnet on the fridge that indicates your habitation in their house, that is a red flag that shouldn't be ignored.
- If you ever find yourself begging the pimply-faced young man at the AT&T store to print off a manuscript of the text conversation between your S.O. and a particular much-texted phone number, prepare to chalk up that relationship as a loss.
- If you make plans with your S.O. and then he/she ghosts you (semi-regularly), later claiming they "forgot their phone," RUN. Run fast and run far.
- If you think I'm crazy and your S.O. isn't like my (former) S.O., well bless your heart and I wish you all the best.

After divorce #3, I met and started dating a fellow Realtor. He was cute with a boyish grin, sparkly blue eyes, and a light smattering of freckles. He was also short, only about an inch taller than me. I think it's worth noting his height, because I really made an exception to date this guy who ultimately took a huge dump on me and contributed to my already long list of trust issues.

He was divorced and was pretty upfront with me about the fact that his cheating had been the main cause of it. We both brought a fair amount of baggage to our relationship but we also both said we wanted to break out of the cycles of our pasts this time around. As far as I knew, we were working together to create a loving, honest connection as well as a kickass real estate team. He was a big proponent of vision boards and "The Secret" and law of attraction. Later, I realized the only thing he was trying to attract was other women... and possibly men.

Now don't misunderstand me here: I don't want that last sentence to be interpreted as "OMG Stacy hates the gays." That couldn't be further from the truth. I am an ally of the LGBTQ community (and whatever other letters I may be missing from that acronym). I hang up my rainbow flag during Pride Month, I'm all about #loveislove, and I've spent many a night at the bar with my gay friends. Hell, once I even had the bright idea to suggest a drag queen as the keynote speaker for a women in business event where the theme was "Real Queens Fix Other Queens' Crowns." (The rest of the committee didn't share my vision, but I still think it was genius.) But as far as the man I'm in a relationship with—I prefer that they're heterosexual.

Extracting myself from that relationship was fairly traumatic. I was living in his house with my autistic son and had hardly any money. I moved into his basement while I waited for the last two real estate transactions we were working on to close. That was in July and the last deal didn't close until September. It was the ickiest sort of limbo, feeling unsafe and unwanted every time I pulled into the driveway and crept quietly into my room in his house. As soon as I had the money from the last commission check (which I had to split 50/50 with him even though I did ninety percent of the work), I found the nicest, most affordable place I could for me and Haiden. We moved in on a rainy day at the beginning of October.

I felt fortunate to have found the two-bedroom home when I did and that the rent was in my budget. It was a charming Craftsman built in 1919, with a gorgeous fireplace, creaky hardwood floors, and old radiator heaters in each room. In the mornings, as I drank my coffee in the small kitchen, I'd sit on top of the heater. When I showered, I'd lay my towel over it so that when I got out I could wrap myself in warmth. These were tiny spots of brightness in what was otherwise a bleak time in my life.

In the darkest hours of my Rock Bottom, there was ONE lifeline, ONE thought that gave me a glimmer of hope about the possibilities for my future: I was a marathon runner. I could do hard shit. Impossible shit. In May of that year I had run my first 26.2-mile race, and at the finish line I found myself a stronger person than I ever imagined. This new idea of myself, this perception of possibilities, the ownership I finally took over my actions and their subsequent consequences, quite legitimately saved my life. For the first time in a long time, I felt a sense of control over my life.

When I started running in 2008, I had no idea I would never stop. I was working for some amazing owners of a local brewery called Roosters when they decided it would be "fun" to put together a few relay teams to run the Ogden Marathon. I was thirty-one at the time and was definitely NOT a runner. In high school when I was in marching band, the punishment for showing up late to practice was running a mile around the track. I NEVER wanted to be late for practice.

I decided (or more like was "voluntold") I would participate on one of the three relay teams. The five-member team would run the entire 26.2-mile race in increments ranging from three to seven miles. I hoped for the shortest portion of three miles but of course when the straws were drawn, I ended up with the first leg of the relay which was the longest. I was completely intimidated by the idea of running seven miles. It literally was unfathomable to me.

I started training. I bought my first pair of "real" running shoes, not from a big box store but a specialty running shop where they threw me on a treadmill and did an analysis of my gait. I bought a hydration belt. I bought expensive socks that promised all sorts of comfort and blister prevention. I started talking to people about running. I started logging miles. I discovered trails and paths by my house (were they really there all along??). I complained to anyone who would listen that I would never run again after I fulfilled my obligation to my team.

The day of the race, I hopped on a bus with my fellow co-workers. The bus made its way through Ogden Canyon for what seemed like a million miles before we were eventually dropped off in a cold, dark field. There were groups huddled around barrels of fire, long lines for the porta-potties, and an energy that I had never experienced.

The announcer warned when we were fifteen minutes from the start of the race. Runners began shedding their layers of warm clothing; they were preparing for a battle I couldn't imagine. Like I said: I was scared of running seven miles and they were about to run three and a half times that! We were herded onto the asphalt, falling into starting spots based on our estimated running pace. The final countdown began, a gun was fired into the chilly spring air, and off we went.

I knew I would average a ten-minute-per-mile pace. This would be my first time running a full seven miles and I felt like it would take forever. I got in my groove: left, right, left, right. Arms swinging. I had never been on this road, so I took in the scenery. Prior to that day, I had heard things about Ogden being ghetto and trashy, but wherever I was, it was anything but. A river gushed by on my left and the smell of bacon and campfire wafted through the trees from nearby campgrounds. I passed the first mile marker. Then the second. Then the third. I was surprised how good I felt, the adrenaline pumping through my body. 'This must be a Runner's

High,' I thought.

The miles continued to tick by. I was starting to hurt but was still enjoying myself. When I got to the relay transition aid station, I ripped the Velcro anklet timing chip off and handed it to my teammate. I was relieved to be finished. I grabbed some water and oranges from a table manned by cheerful, energetic volunteers and hobbled toward the bus that would take the relay runners down to the finish line. I was feeling sore, accomplished, and REALLY proud of myself. Until we started riding back through the canyon and I saw all the marathoners.

There was one runner in particular— he was wearing a tutu and a headband with bright red braids so that he looked like the girl on the Wendy's restaurant logo. I thought he was both amazing and incredibly stupid, all at once. Why would anyone run 26.2 miles, especially in that getup?? (Full disclosure: I have since run a marathon in a tutu. It's not so bad.)

When the bus dropped us off in downtown Ogden, still with no sign of the so-called ghetto, we made our way to the crowd of cheering spectators at the finish line. Someone handed me a cowbell and I joined in with the shouting of encouragement to the runners. It dawned on me that I had done the longest portion of the relay run, and I wouldn't have the chance to enjoy the feeling of crossing the finish line.

I could tell there was magic in that finish line. I saw it on the face of every person who passed by me. Men, women, young, old, every shape, size and color. It didn't matter. When they crossed that finish line, they were triumphant. There were chafed, bloody nipples, runners who vomited, and tears, both of pain and glory. I was covered in goosebumps as tears rolled down my cheeks. I wanted to know what that magic felt like. I wanted to cross a marathon finish line.

The following year in 2009, I did just that. And I *found myself* at that finish line. At the time I said I would only do one; I have since done eight full marathons, countless half marathons, an ultra-marathon 50K, three triathlons, and eight Ragnar Relays. I volunteered as an ambassador for the Ogden Marathon, promoting it on my social media and offering a discount code for others to use when they registered. Running changed my entire life for the better. Through running, I met many amazing people. One of those people was a guy named Kyle.

I met Kyle on a late summer evening in 2016 at the Lighthouse Lounge on Historic 25th Street in Ogden. I had been running with a group for just over a year, meeting once a week at a local bar where we would run three miles and then convene for a frosty beverage and socializing shenanigans. He was a newcomer to the group but with his outgoing personality and friendly smile, no one would have ever known. He quickly became a regular and everyone was smitten by him. Kyle's effervescent personality naturally drew people to him. He was fit, tan, and lean with a head of beautiful blonde, wavy locks and bright blue eyes. But even more than his boyish good looks, Kyle had a heart of gold.

In December that year, I had heard about an idea called the "Burrito Project," where a group would get together to roll burritos and take them out to feed the homeless in their community. I invited some friends to participate in our own version of this project. About a dozen people showed up to my house that chilly morning with their assigned breakfast burrito fillings, ready to assemble. Kyle showed up with dozens of scrambled eggs and a huge bag of sauce packets from a local Mexican fast food joint.

"I told them what we were doing, and they just gave these all to me," he said, with a smile and a shrug.

We rolled over a hundred burritos that day and then hit the streets, passing them out to gracious souls in our community. Afterward, Kyle and I ran back to my house. We made small talk as we ran, mostly about our past and future runs. I was surprised to find out he had very recently began running, especially considering what great shape he was in. I was even more shocked when he told me how he had quit a 22-year smoking habit. That was one of the first of many runs, talks and adventures I would share with this new friend.

If there was fun to be had, not only was Kyle there, but he was usually the mastermind. He created a new sect for our running group called Ogden Trail Troopers. Because road runs could get monotonous and hard on joints, he initiated runs on the beautiful mountain trails. He kayaked, went to concerts, mountain biked, and ran. He threw parties at his house, cooked amazing meals, and helped anyone in need.

He owned his own electrical company and once, when our dining room fixture broke, he came over to take a look at it. When he checked one of the light bulbs, it exploded and burst into flame. He wasn't even fazed and kept going about his work. We ended up needing a new fixture, which he procured and replaced, free of charge. He also served on the board of a shelter for at-risk youth and when they built a second location, he did all their electrical work pro bono as well. Never mind that he drove over five hours down and back every weekend for months. He worked hard and played even harder.

In February of 2017 he announced that he wanted to do the Grand Circle Trailfest in October that year, a series of back-to-back trail runs at Bryce, Zion, and the Grand Canyon, totaling more than forty miles altogether. Since I had recently experienced the death of my ex-husband Stacey, I desperately felt the need to do something big, bigger than myself. I took a deep breath, ignoring the panic at paying almost six hundred dollars for a race, and signed up.

Not long after we had registered, Kyle tore his ACL. He took the absolute minimum time he possibly could to recuperate and rehab. In May, despite everyone trying to talk him out of it, he ran the Ogden marathon. I knew he was a faster, stronger runner than me, even in a knee brace. The morning of the run, we loaded onto the VIP bus, making our usual jokes about pooping and pre-race jitters. He told me he would stick with me for the whole 26.2-mile race.

"Please don't," I told him. "I don't want to slow you down."

"It's fine," he said. "I need you to make sure I don't overdo it."

True to his word, he stayed with me the entire time. At mile thirteen I slowed down to eat an energy bar. I begged him to go ahead. He would not. At mile seventeen I stopped at a Honey Bucket for a potty break. He was patiently, loyally waiting for me when I popped back out. Through Ogden Canyon, along the parkway, up until the last block of the finish line. He pulled, pushed, and prodded me when I wanted to give up. A few steps from the finish line, he placed his hand on the small of my back and pushed me ahead, so that I crossed the finish line before him.

Kyle's knee was still giving him trouble, but that didn't stop him from coming to the Grand Circle Trailfest in October. He would decide once we were there if he felt like he was up for doing any of the runs. On the drive down, we talked about our pasts; Kyle sharing stories of being a homeless youth and overcoming drug addiction. I shared my own story of surviving childhood sexual abuse. I thought to myself how amazing my tribe of badass friends was and how lucky I had been to find them.

We got to the race headquarters and set up in the "tent city." Our group of friends formed a circle in between our two tents with our chairs, and the boys popped beers while the girls poured mimosas. In the evening, Kyle lit a cigar. I laughed as people walked by and gave him dirty looks. If I knew nothing else about Kyle, I knew that he didn't give a shit what others thought about him. It was one of his most endearing qualities.

He opted out of the first race, a grueling 14-mile run at Bryce Canyon. While the rest of us ran, he rode his bike around the park in the chilly weather. But at the finish line, like the beacon of a lighthouse, he was always there for us. That first run kicked my ass and I seriously contemplated not running the next two. Kyle wouldn't have it and told me he would even run the second race. The next day, a 13ish-mile run at Zion Canyon, he threw on his running gear and joined us. Even with his knee in a brace, he finished before me. When I got to the finish line, my entire group of friends was there waiting for me.

On the final run at the Grand Canyon, Kyle dropped us off at the start line and headed out on his mountain bike. Everyone else was ahead of me as I climbed the first five miles of the challenging course. When I finally made it to the top and it leveled out to a dirt road, I picked up my pace. I saw a familiar shape in the distance and was elated when I realized it was Kyle on the trail. I popped out my earbuds.

"Hi, buddy!" I shouted.

"How's it going?" he asked cheerfully.

"I'm ready for a mimosa," I replied.

"I'll have it ready for you when you're finished," he said, flashing his bright Kyle smile.

Sure enough, when I finally made it across the finish line and over to Kyle's truck "Big Red," he was sitting in the bed, smoking his cigar, and he handed me a cup of champagne and OJ. I gulped down the first cup, the bubbles going straight to my head. I poured myself another one and sipped, feeling a sense of warm, accomplished euphoria. Shortly after, we went back to race HQ, packed up our belongings, and headed home.

In 2017, I was asked to serve on the board of the running group. I was hesitant, only because I had a lot going on with Haiden and Eli as well as a lot of other commitments I worried would stretch me thin. However, since I loved the group and I didn't think it would be a huge time commitment, I said yes. A few months later, some more awesome friends joined the board and I was thrilled at how amazing they all would be. One of the new board members was Kyle. I felt comfortable in the knowledge that these people were my tribe.

Kyle had been really busy, so we didn't think much of it when he didn't show up for a lot of our group runs, or he missed a board meeting. Not only was he was serving on the GOAL Foundation and helping out a ton getting ready for the 2018 Ogden Marathon, but that was when he was making the drive to St. George every weekend to do the electrical work on the youth shelter. That was the kind of person he was. Despite being so busy and not having a ton of time to train, he still ran the Ogden Marathon on May 19th. He rode the VIP bus to the start line with my husband, and they casually chatted on the way up.

I only ran the half marathon that year, so when I got to the finish line, I had plenty of time to relax while I waited for my hubby and the rest of our friends. The spectator festivities were in full swing by the time the full marathoners were finishing. We saw Kyle as he neared the finish, and we burst into celebratory screams, handing him an ice-cold beer which he raised over his head and carried, like an Olympic torch, as he crossed the finish line. He made his way over to our group where we showered him with praise and accolades for a job well done. He was tired, naturally, and only celebrated with us for a little while before excusing himself and heading home. We were having a board dinner that night, but he messaged us to tell us he was too tired to come. I didn't realize then that would be the last day I would ever see Kyle again.

In the two years I had known Kyle, he had been very active on social media. I realized, since the marathon, that I hadn't heard or seen too much from him. I went to his Facebook profile one day and saw that the last post he made was from the marathon on May 19th, almost two weeks prior. I was perplexed, but I figured, in true Kyle fashion, he was just really busy. I thought about sending him a text to let him know I was thinking about him but never did. A couple days later, he commented on a post I had made about doing a race in Moab in November.

"Ahh, he's back," I thought. Whatever qualms I had were quieted.

***

On the morning of June 7[th,] I had just finished setting up my marketing stuff on Hole One of the miniature golf course at Toad's Fun Zone for my job as a home warranty rep. I was wearing a black running skort and Rainbow Brite socks as part of my gimmicky marketing. This is how everyone knew me: funny, silly Stacy. Over the years I had dressed up in costumes for work events in everything from Princess Leia to Napoleon Dynamite to a margarita. It was one of the most fun work perks and a throwback to my bartending days.

I glanced at my phone and saw that I had missed a call from Dusty. He sent an ominous text: "Call me as soon as you can."

I immediately thought something had happened to his dad. A few weeks prior, I was alarmed when Papa Frank took us out to dinner and asked multiple times, "So, anything new going on with you?" It was like watching *Groundhog Day*, and it was incredibly unnerving.

I called Dusty, bracing for the bad news about Papa.

"Have you been on Facebook?" he asked, his voice low.

"Not since earlier this morning," I replied, confused at his line of questioning. What did this have to do with his dad?

"Babe," he whispered. "I don't know how to tell you this…"

"What?"

"Kyle," he whispered. "Kyle killed himself. It's all over Facebook."

I know that there was a chemical reaction happening in my brain, that this message was being interpreted, packaged up and sent to its respective place. But the connection between the synapses was failing. It was nonsense what my husband was saying. The words traveled to my ears as if from somewhere very far away, and I couldn't comprehend it. I knew he had to be mistaken.

"What?" I know I mustn't have heard him right. My brain was telling me NO NO NO, this is not right. The world was spinning. My vision blurred with tears. I stood, stupidly, ridiculous in my cheerful multi-colored knee-high socks, shrieking. I heard and felt the sound escaping me, but I had no control over it. The crowd of people around me laughed and joked as they headed out to start miniature golfing, oblivious to the fact that the world had momentarily halted its spinning. A few of them noticed me falling apart and swept in to help keep me together.

"I'm coming home," Dusty said, as I realized I was still holding my phone to my ear.

I was hysterical. Someone gently led me inside to a table in the arcade area. Arms embraced me; someone handed me a bottle of water and tissues; I messaged the rest of the board members from the running group. What do we do? This can't be real; this can't be happening; THIS CAN'T BE KYLE.

News of Kyle's suicide spread quickly and shocked the community in which he was an active part. Our running group held its weekly run that Thursday evening, and it was somber. It was as if everyone felt that there was a pause in the goings on of the world, yet life continued. There was a huge outdoor concert that evening, a concert Kyle should have been attending. There was a new reality of life as we knew it, before and after Kyle. The refrain we heard over and over in the coming days from every circle he ran in was: "We never saw it coming."

Kyle's light was extinguished on June 6th, 2018, the same week as Kate Spade on the 5th, and Anthony Bourdain on the 8th. The entire nation, it seemed, was rocked by the shock and sadness surrounding the celebrities' suicides. Social media was inundated with suicide awareness memes, suicide hotline phone numbers, and messages of "GET HELP." I too felt a certain amount of melancholy about them, but I was completely devastated by the loss of my friend. His death left behind two teenage sons, eleven days before one of their birthdays and Father's Day. Three local non-profits lost a beloved board member. A family lost a son, brother, uncle. I lost one of my best friends.

I have replayed every conversation, every run, every encounter I ever had with Kyle, searching for the clues that I must have missed. I come up empty-handed and more heartbroken every time. I think of how adventurous he was— was it recklessness? I remember how he didn't wear his seatbelt on our drive to Kanab— was that an indication of wanting to die? I never saw signs of depression; I never thought Kyle was in or could go to a place where suicide was a viable option for him; and I was at a loss as to why that's the way his life ended. An unbearable ache filled my chest every day.

**

The night in November 2009 that I vividly recall as the very rockiest bottom of my "Rock Bottom," I drank a bottle of wine and decided to take a bath. I loved the large bathroom of the adorable Craftsman home I rented, with its built-in cabinets and hexagon-tiled floor. I had decorated it with thrift store finds, so everything was mismatched and whimsical. As the bathtub filled with steaming hot water and bubbles, I opened my medicine cabinet and found a bottle with a few tiny white pills. I didn't know what they were, but I decided I would take them along with another bottle of wine I had just uncorked.

I slid into the hot water, daring myself to go under the surface. Tears streamed down my face as feelings of worthlessness, hopelessness and despair engulfed me. My life in that moment was a shit show and that was pretty much the best it would ever be. My kids would be better off without me; my whole family would be. I wanted to shrink into myself and dissolve into the hot bath water. I just wanted to stop hurting. I leaned my head back and waited for the wine and pills to do their job, so I could carelessly slip below the water's surface. The oblivion never came. Hell, maybe those pills had been baby Tylenol.

After some time, as the water cooled, I groggily pulled the plug and sobbed as the water noisily swirled down the drain. I pulled myself out of the tub and curled into the fetal position, naked on the cheerful floor mat that looked like a goldfish bowl. I knew in that moment I wasn't ready to end my life, but I sure as shit needed to do something to change it.

***

I thought the marathon saved people. I thought this tribe, this one percent of the population, was unbreakable. I naively thought all the running endorphins could help cure everything. I thought I was impervious to heartbreak. Kyle proved me wrong on all counts. I don't know what demons he fought but he must have given them a hell of a fight for as long as he could. The Kyle I knew was strong, resilient, a fighter, a survivor. He was like me. When we got pushed down, we got back up, dusted ourselves off, and got our asses back in the arena. He was a Success Story, a Golden Boy, a Warrior. He was a light everywhere he went. Until he wasn't.

A few weeks after his death, I got inked with a tattoo I had wanted for months: a compass with mountains in the center and a feather along the bottom. This tattoo represented all the ways I had found myself on the trails, especially when I ran my first 50K ultra-marathon at Antelope Island in November of 2017; Kyle had been there to cheer and had even gotten a video of me and my two friends as we crossed the finish line, arms raised in victory, just like he always did. When I asked the tattoo artist if he could incorporate a semicolon, the symbol for suicide awareness, into my tattoo he replied, "Hell yeah. We can create the shape in the negative space in the stars over the mountains." I found it a perfect parallel, knowing that Kyle would forever exist "in the negative space." Kyle was gone, but I couldn't accept that his story was over. I knew I would find him on the trails, and I trusted that he would continue to help me as I found my way.

Months after Kyle died, I continued to struggle with overwhelming emotions I had not anticipated. I had many in-depth conversations with a handful of friends who felt similarly; one had gone to a medium and when she shared her experience with me, I cried hearing about all the messages Kyle had given her. What I was most surprised to discover, however, was that many people within Kyle's circle, his running tribe, seemed to have put an expiration date on the amount of time they were willing to spend mourning him.

In the fall, as we planned our annual fundraiser, we discussed paying tribute to Kyle at the event. A few of the board members bristled at the idea, saying that they didn't want to put a damper on the evening's festivities. I had assumed that we were all on the same page and I was shocked when I realized we weren't even on the same chapter. I didn't feel like Kyle "made the decision to leave, so we shouldn't glorify him." People in the community looked to us as Kyle's tribe, and sitting in on that conversation felt like a betrayal to him and everyone who loved him. It was as if his death, that singular, horrible instant now defined his entire life.

His death has served as a reminder to me to live my best life, purposefully and passionately. Kyle lived adventurously, authentically, and generously. My life is better for having known him. I believe he is with me; I believe he wants to see me succeed, and I think he would be happy to read these words about himself. I hope I am honoring him and that his family takes some comfort in the small but impactful piece he has added to my story. I hope by sharing his story, it helps someone else who needs to hear it.

Kyle has sent me some signs, letting me know he is looking out for me. I started looking for feathers after Stacey died, a sign from the Universe from my angels. When I find them now— on runs, mostly, but also at other random times— I feel like Kyle is telling me to keep up what I'm doing, and that I'm on the right path. It's funny how, when you start looking for something, you somehow manage to find it at the moment you need it most. I've run many miles carrying his memory in my heart. As I neared the end of 2018, the year that he died, I focused on what the new year would bring. I had a lot of big, somewhat lofty goals and I was both excited and absolutely terrified about how I was going to achieve them.

One Sunday morning, I received an invitation to speak at an event in Texas and I was so elated that I skipped over some of the details of the email. I went for a quick run and came home, excitedly waiting to tell Dusty the news. I opened the email and began to read it out loud when the words caught in my throat. My friend Dena had written:

"Stacy,

I've been thinking a lot about you and following your journey on Instagram. I'm really excited for you. I'm excited for me too since we're on such similar trajectories. I went a little crazy the other day and decided to book a venue and host my first ever live women's event. It is going to be held the afternoon of January 6, 2019 in Kyle, TX… I think that you would be a perfect fit for a near-final keynote at the event…"

I looked up at Dusty. He was staring at me.

"Oh my gosh," I said. "Kyle, TX?"

"Think it's a sign?" he asked.

"Hell yes, I do!"

I don't believe in coincidence, especially one that put me in a town and on a stage exactly seven months after his death, where I was literally surrounded by signs that read "Kyle." It was almost comical and I wouldn't have expected anything less from him. I met Kyle for reasons I didn't know at the time. His story has become part of my story, and I intend to keep his memory alive for many more years to come.

I wish with everything that I am that he had been able to weather the storm; that he could have seen that there was light after the darkness. Because here's the kicker, the hardest most bitter pill to swallow about this whole suicide thing: If sweet, kind, resilient, buoyant, superhuman Kyle could succumb to a feeling, a persistent nagging voice in his head, that told him the world was better without him, then what did that mean for the rest of us mere mortals?

I have text messages between me and Kyle that I can't bring myself to erase off my phone. Pretty much every exchange was me asking for some sort of favor: a picture he had taken on our run that day; an electrical question; a running question; and more electrical questions. The last text I sent him was on March 26, 2018, less than two and a half months before he died. Why hadn't I checked in on him when I noticed he was M.I.A. on Facebook? It would have taken ten seconds for me to send him a message. I don't know that it would have changed anything, but as a resident in the Land of the Living, it's one less regret I would have had, letting him know I was thinking about him.

I sometimes look at my own reflection in the mirror and see the stressed-out mom, wife, woman looking back at me. And I think to myself, "What makes me think I'm stronger than Kyle?" I go back to that night in November, when I toed the ledge of my own personal hell. All it would have taken was a few seconds for my fate to have taken a different turn. What the hell was Kyle thinking in those final moments of his life that he extinguished the bright light he was in so many people's lives? The world without him is a little dimmer. And I find myself in the strangest of places, a marathon relay of sorts, where Kyle has passed the baton to me, and I am tasked with carrying it to the finish line.

*This story has been adapted from its original post on my blog on June 20, 2018 and published here with permission from Kyle's family.

**If you or anyone you know is struggling with depression or suicidal thoughts, please GET HELP NOW. Your story isn't over. There is hope.

National Suicide Prevention Lifeline 1.800.273.8255 (US)

CHAPTER FOUR:
CHILDHOOD SEXUAL ABUSE
(AND LOSING MY RELIGION)

"Shame cannot survive being spoken. It cannot tolerate having words wrapped around it. What it craves is secrecy, silence, and judgment. If you stay quiet, you stay in a lot of self-judgment."
~Brené Brown, *Daring Greatly*

My grandmother once spent hours cutting, piecing together, and sewing matching Strawberry Shortcake rompers for me and my older sister. Years later, when our tastes had matured and we had outgrown the rompers, my mom would take us shopping for clothes patterns and material, and she too would spend hours sewing outfits for us. I loved these pieces, knowing they were made precisely to my measurements, with cloth that I handpicked. It never dawned on me that these homemade garments were a necessity not a frivolity, that it was the only way my mom could afford for us to have new clothes for the school year. After my parents divorced and my mom had to move us into a trailer, I finally realized we were officially poor.

My mom put on a brave face and never let on how tight things were. She bought powdered milk that she mixed in the regular milk jug, hoping we wouldn't notice the difference. We did, but we drank it anyway. We learned how to fry bologna for sandwiches, make Eggs-in-a-Hole, and a variety of ways to dress up ramen noodles. We clipped coupons and took them to Phar-Mor where they doubled the face value, doubling our savings. We bought generic everything, in bulk. I learned that name brand stuff was a luxury and one which we could not afford. I didn't mind, really, except on the few occasions all my friends seemed to be wearing Keds or L.A. Gear, and I felt like the only one sporting ugly knockoffs.

For Easter she wanted me and Christy to have new dresses to wear to church. I thought the Kmart dress she proudly pulled out of the bag was hideous, but when I saw the five-dollar clearance sticker, I shut my mouth. I knew those dresses, plus the outfits she had gotten for our younger brothers, were a splurge.

In eighth grade I was invited to the end-of-the-year dance by a trombone player from band class who I had a crush on. I desperately wanted a new dress but my mom was too busy with work and nursing school classes to sew one for me. She gave me a teeny tiny budget, and we set off in search of an affordable and elegant dress. I started with all the stores at the mall and came up empty-handed. On the way home, we passed a strip mall and I saw a sign for a thrift consignment store. We pulled into the parking lot, and I was feeling both dismayed and hopeful about the store's prospects.

The store smelled a little musty and moth-bally and was jam-packed full of treasures. I found the rack of women's dresses and started my search. My heart pounded in excitement when a burgundy dress caught my eye. I pulled it off the rack and held it up in front of me, inspecting it for any obvious flaws. Not seeing any, I nearly skipped to the dressing room. I hurriedly undressed, slid the dress off its hanger, and stepped in. I zipped it up and turned to look in the mirror. It was taffeta with three ruffles that comprised the skirt, a heart-shaped bodice covered in matching lace, a giant bow at the waistline, and generously puffy sleeves. It was magnificent, and even better: it was in my price range.

I fell in love with thrifting. The thrill of finding a bargain, the treasure of another person's trash, was exhilarating. Consignment stores, yard sales, and estate sales became my shopping venues of choice. Sometimes I bought name brand apparel, but it was never the focus of my bargain hunting. I liked what I liked, which tended to be somewhat loud and funky, and it didn't matter to me what the name was on the label. I was proud of my frugality, and when I got complimented on my finds I would boast, "Yes, and it was only five dollars!"

The gift of thrift came in handy over the years, as I wove in and out of bad marriages and therefore in and out of money. I was grateful for having grown up poor because it prepared me for years of being broke. So, as an adult, it became somewhat absurd that I wore secondhand clothes and I started carrying expensive, name brand purses. If you've ever been at a store checkout judging the mom in front of you who's holding a Coach wallet while paying for her groceries with food stamps, well that woman might have been me. And maybe what you'll never know is the story leading up to that woman who feels so utterly broken and ashamed, embarrassed to be on government assistance, ironically holding a wallet worth more than she currently has in her bank account. Her story might be similar to mine.

I hadn't had much of a relationship with my father since I was about fifteen. After my parents divorced, he moved to a neighboring town for a couple years and then he moved out of the state. I wasn't sad about it, him leaving; he was a memory to me by that point anyway, a shadow of someone I just used to know. He could have lived five miles away or five thousand miles away, and it wouldn't have made much difference. We never spoke, and the only time he seemed to think of any of his kids was on birthdays and when he sent gifts at Christmas. He simply became a representation of the man we formerly called Dad.

He used to email us, inquiring about what we and our kids had on our holiday wish list. At some point that must have become too tedious for him and he set up what seemed to be a subscription on auto-renewal. Each year, we'd receive a tin of food items from a company called Swiss Colony. Sometimes cheeses and sausages would show up in festive red and gold boxes; other times mini petit fours cakes in a variety of bite-size flavors. The worst was when he'd send trays of dried fruit—blech.

And to me and my two sisters, he started sending name brand purses or wallets. Dooney and Burke, Coach, Ralph Lauren, and Kate Spade. Some of them I used, some I consigned, some collected dust in my closet. All of them stirred up in me a quiet rage. I felt like they were bought with hush money and they were thoughtless, just as my dad had been to my mom and our family.

***

For most of my life, I wasn't vocal about my abuse. I knew that no one was interested in hearing about my damaged, broken parts. One time, in my early thirties, I was on a date with a super manly macho military guy. As we drove down the interstate toward the restaurant he had chosen, he offhandedly said, "There's something wrong with girls who join the military. Every girl in the military has 'daddy issues.'" I laughed and pasted on what felt like the fakest of fake smiles as I made a mental note not to bring up my own "daddy issues." He was not the first, nor would he be the last, to subtly silence and shame me.

I don't know how long my abuse lasted because I couldn't pinpoint exactly when it began. The memories around that time were fuzzy, blurred by the confusion of whether or not my dad's actions were inappropriate. He would ask me to put on my bathing suit and then take pictures of me, posing awkwardly in our living room. It felt weird, but was it abuse? I had recently started shaving my legs and once, after showering as I headed to my room wrapped in a towel, my dad stopped me.

"Come here," he said. "I'll put lotion on your legs." He patted the spot next to him on the couch in our family room. I felt obligated to obey him and extremely uncomfortable as he lathered overly sweet-smelling lotion on my newly smooth legs. As soon as he was finished, I hurried to the safety of the room I shared with my older sister. I debated whether to say something to her about it, but decided it probably wasn't a big deal. Dads can rub lotion on their teenage daughter's legs, right?

My dad was in the Navy, so he was often gone for long periods of time, out to sea on his submarine, the USS Francis Scott Key. I was so enamored with his stint in the service that in third grade I wrote a report on and learned about the life of Francis Scott Key. Mr. Key had written a poem that would later become the words to "The Star-Spangled Banner." Knowing my dad was on that submarine filled me with so much pride. With him gone as much as he was, it sometimes felt like we were raised by a single mom. My mom was strong during every deployment, making it look easy raising two, then three, then four kids by herself. When my dad came home, our house was filled with celebratory vibes, and my siblings and I yearned for his attention and affection as if it was in limited supply. He was like the sun and we all wanted to bask in his rays.

He was creative and artistic, dabbling in painting and drawing and playing the guitar. He was a good cook, concocting all types of meat and veggie stir fry dishes that he'd serve with steaming white rice and sliced tomatoes. His laughter was a melodious baritone that Christy and I competed for. He had dark brown skin, jet black hair, a neatly trimmed mustache, and a heart-shaped tattoo on his arm inked with the word 'Mom.' When we tried to get our way and our parents played Good Cop, Bad Cop, our dad was *always* the Good Cop.

I didn't know what the normal daddy/daughter dynamics were supposed to be. Once, while sitting in our Mormon church meeting on a Sunday morning, I watched a family a few rows ahead of us. The dad reached over to his teenage daughter's back and massaged her shoulders with his right hand. He kneaded her neck and the nape of her hairline. I watched, transfixed, and my skin crawled. I wanted to yell, "Stop that! Stop *touching* her!" I didn't know if I was wrong for thinking and feeling that way, but I was repulsed.

We moved often with the military, almost yearly. From New Jersey to Cuba, Pennsylvania, California, Virginia, and finally South Carolina. Since we had moved around so much, we either rented an apartment or lived in base housing. It wasn't until I was in third grade and we knew we'd be stationed there for a while that my parents decided to build a house in the up-and-coming St. James Estates III neighborhood in Goose Creek. We moved in right before I started fourth grade, and my sister and I quickly went about meeting all the other neighborhood kids.

Because we were Mormon, we usually struggled finding and making friends who weren't also Mormon. They tended to look at us like we were two-headed freaks, a notion I'm sure their parents passed down to them about "those people praying to that Joseph Smith guy." But when we moved into the new house it was on a cul-de-sac and boys would bring their small skateboard ramps over right in front of our house, so it was pretty easy making friends when our street was THE place to be.

I loved that house in that neighborhood. It was the first time we lived somewhere that was *ours*. We roamed the wooded area that separated our subdivision from the next. We played in the small creek and the large sewer pipes that ran under our streets. We rode our bikes along every street, we stayed out late on summer evenings, and we toured the destruction caused by the small tornado that ripped through our neighborhood during Hurricane Hugo. We got a cat and hamsters. My dad built a large bench swing in the backyard where we hung out with friends. Our next-door neighbor had a pontoon boat parked in their driveway where we spent hours onboard, sailing the imaginary world. And while my days were filled with friends and innocent fun, my nights became a time filled with dread.

Our house was a chocolate-colored, split-level with three bedrooms upstairs and one bedroom downstairs. When we had first moved in, I had my own room upstairs along with my brother Alex and my parents. My sister Christy was in the downstairs bedroom, and there was a family room and the laundry room down there as well. When my baby brother Josh was born, I got booted from my upstairs bedroom and joined my sister downstairs. Since the family room and laundry room were downstairs, it wasn't uncommon to hear my mom or dad watching TV or folding a load of laundry after we had gone to bed.

One night, I woke up to the startling sensation of someone touching me. I blinked in the darkness, lying in that space of half-awake, half-asleep, not sure if what I had felt was real. On the side of the waterbed that I shared with Christy, I saw my dad crouched down underneath the window. The moon shined in through the blinds and I saw his white undergarments against his dark skin. I felt frozen with terror. Startled, I whispered, "Dad?" He lifted his index finger to his mouth, giving the universal sign for "Shhh." He slowly crept out of my room. Trembling, I looked at my sleeping sister. Whatever lingering doubts I had had about what was or was not inappropriate between a father and daughter, in that moment I knew with certainty that this was definitely NOT appropriate.

The next day I watched my dad's every move. As he mowed the lawn, I peeked through the blinds at him. I don't know what I was looking for—some sign, an acknowledgement, a wink? I wondered if he would say anything to me, give me some explanation for why he had been in my room. I wondered if I would believe him, whatever excuse he may have had. But nothing ever came. He didn't act any differently toward me, he didn't apologize, nothing. I started thinking that maybe I had dreamt the whole thing. I found comfort in this thought, so I clung to it. And just when I had convinced myself that it had been my imagination, it happened again.

It didn't happen every night and there didn't seem to be a pattern. I would study him at the dinner table, searching for some sign of the insidious man who showed up in my room. He acted so *normal*, laughing and joking with everyone. Our family dinners had always been a time of happiness for us, first in the preparation when mom would ask me to make the salad. I'd cut up the vegetables and place them on top of the bowl of lettuce in pretty patterns or a funny face.

Then around the table as we'd all talk about our days. No one would have ever guessed that my charismatic father was such a wolf in sheep's clothing. As he put on his game of charades, I silently played along with him, an unwilling accomplice to his crimes.

Every night I prayed that he wouldn't show up in my room. Sometimes my prayers were answered; other nights they were not. I felt like I never quite allowed myself to fall into deep sleep, that part of my consciousness was always at alert. I possessed a Spidey-sense, my eyes snapped open when I felt his presence enter my room. I'd catch a glimpse of the flash of white of his garments out of the corner of my eye and my blood froze in my veins as my heart hammered in my chest. He seemed to linger longer if I was still, presumably thinking I was asleep, so I learned if I rolled over or otherwise stirred, he usually pulled back and retreated from my room.

I felt very alone. Who could I possibly tell? My own sister slept soundly right next to me—would she have believed me if I told her? One night I tried locking our bedroom door. My mom, who was on her way upstairs from doing laundry, tried to open the door and yelled, "Why is this locked?" I unlocked it and mumbled an excuse about what if robbers broke into our house? Wouldn't she want us to be safe? She rolled her eyes. "It's a fire hazard," she said. "Don't lock your door." I wanted to tell her I would rather burn to the ground with the house than have my dad sneak in while everyone else slept peacefully, oblivious to my personal hell.

When I was in sixth grade, my mom went to her youngest sister's wedding in New Jersey. Usually our entire family would have made the trip but my mom didn't want us missing school, so she made the trip solo. When she came back a few days later and we picked her up from the airport, I immediately sensed that something was wrong. She was quiet the whole way home and then during dinner. Afterward she told me and my sister to go downstairs. Christy glanced at me nervously. When we sat down and sloshed around on the waterbed, she asked me if I knew what was going on with mom. "I think I have an idea of what it might be," I said. "But let's wait until she comes down here." We could hear her yelling upstairs. A little while later, she knocked on our door.

There aren't very many conversations from my youth that I can recall with great detail, but the one we had with our mom that night is one of them. When she came into our room, her eyes were bloodshot and more tired than I had ever seen them. She sat down with us, the bed jostling us around. She took a long, slow breath. We stared at her, wide-eyed, knowing that a bomb was about to drop.

"I need to know if your father has ever… done anything to you." Her lips quavered. Christy looked dumbfounded. "No! What do you mean?" I was relieved to hear that he hadn't done anything to her, too; but I dreaded what I was about to tell my mom. Her eyes drifted from Christy's shocked face to mine. I looked away for a second.

"Stacy? Has he done anything to you?" Her voice cracked on the question.

Finally. This weight I had silently shouldered for years was about to be let go. But as much as I was relieved to be unburdening it, I didn't want to transfer all that weight onto my mom. I hesitated and swallowed, saddened about what I was about to say to my mom about her husband.

"Yes," I whispered.

Christy looked at me, a shocked expression on her face.

"For how long?" my mom asked. Her voice was heavy with anguish and her eyes filled with tears.

"I'm not sure, exactly. A while."

She breathed heavily, shakily. "Why didn't you tell me?"

"I didn't think you'd believe me," I whispered. I asked her a question I hadn't even consciously realized I had: "Is Danny our brother?"

My mom looked as surprised by the question as I felt asking it. Danny was our cousin by my mom's older sister. My aunt, who had never married or been in a serious relationship that anyone knew of, had always been pretty mysterious about the father of the son she had had four years earlier. She was a nurse and had told everyone the father was a doctor at the hospital where she worked. No one seemed to question this, nor did they question the fact that her baby was brown-skinned and resembled me and my siblings. Somehow, I connected the dots. My mom nodded, tight-lipped as more tears continued to stream down her cheeks.

She told us that her family had taken the opportunity, while my dad wasn't around, to sit her down and tell her *everything* he had been doing, for *years*. It had gone on for so long that if they had told her when it first started, maybe she could have saved it from happening to me. I felt both relief and grief in that moment. Glad I no longer had to carry around this heavy secret, relieved that my voice wasn't the only one speaking out against my dad and I wouldn't have to "prove" my case to be believed by anyone, and heartbroken for my mom having to deal with her world crashing around her. That conversation would be the first of many where my mom no longer spoke to us like children; we were forced to grow up and face some hard realities in that moment.

Not sure what to do about her unraveling marriage to my dad, she approached the leaders of our church. She told them about his years of extramarital affairs, his sexual advances on almost every one of her sisters, and his abuse against me. The church leaders counseled her to forgive him, salvage the marriage at all costs, and that if she couldn't fulfill these obligations, then she was the bigger sinner in the eyes of the Lord.

I'm gonna say that a little louder for those at the back of the room: IF SHE DIDN'T FORGIVE A CHEATING, ADULTERING PEDOPHILE, SHE WOULD BE THE BIGGER SINNER.

At the end of the meeting, they bestowed a blessing upon my mom and sent her on her way. When she came home that night, stricken and broken, and told me what the leaders had instructed, I was shocked. I didn't understand why they would tell her such a thing. When I was in fourth grade, in a portable unit at Howe Hall Elementary with Mr. Hauser, a Vietnam Vet, as my teacher, the school secretary's voice crackled over the intercom speaker one day.

"Are Stacy and Mary in class today?" she asked.

Mr. Hauser confirmed our presence, a confused expression on his face. Mary and I looked at each other quizzically. She was a pretty half-Filipino girl with long, wavy hair and big, brown eyes. I shrugged and giggled, then went back to working on my spelling words. Later, I asked my mom why the secretary had been looking for us. Hesitantly, she explained that both she and Mary's mom had received a phone call from a man who said he had abducted us from the school playground. We never found out who had made the calls, or why he had targeted us. But I knew that if he had ever been caught, his ass would have been grass and the Goose Creek Police Department would have been the mower.

Knowing that, I couldn't reconcile that what my dad had done wasn't a criminal offense. If someone could get in trouble simply for making a threatening phone call, well what my dad had done was way worse than that. Why wasn't GCPD at our house? Where was the concern from the school staff about my wellbeing? Why wasn't someone coming to help me? Where was the outrage from the male, trusted leaders of our church? Why were they protecting my dad? I couldn't grasp that this was God's will. At thirteen, I lost faith in the only religion I had ever known. The patriarchal Mormon church and its leaders failed me and my family and protected a predator. My voice was silenced, my story was stifled.

As part of, what I'm sure the church leaders thought was a good idea for, my healing process, I started having sessions with a therapist. They kindly referred my mom to someone who was well-versed in situations like ours. He was a heavyset man who attended our church but was in a different "ward," which was Mormon-speak for congregation. I recognized him from the times our ward schedules overlapped at the church building and I'd see him in the hallway.

In our sessions, I felt an overwhelmingly cringy discomfort, hyper aware of being alone in a room with a man, whose heavy breathing hung in the silent air I was expected to fill with the details of my abuse. I'd grip the arms of the chair I sat in opposite him, feeling beads of nervous sweat drip from my armpits down the backs of my arm. The time dragged on in the slowest of slow motion; time that I knew was a waste since this "therapy" was little more than a display that the church leaders had done their due diligence. They had swept my abuse under the rug, and this was just one of their last steps in tidying up behind themselves.

For the next year, while my mom barely kept her own shit together, she tried valiantly to be an obedient Mormon wife and fought to keep the family together. We heard her crying almost every night. She slept on the couch in the upstairs living room, afraid my dad would try to sneak down to our room. She battled depression and, she later admitted, thoughts of suicide. Our home felt like a war zone. On Sundays, we schlepped through the motions and made our appearance at church, but the resentment I felt steadily grew with each passing week.

I'd watch as the teenage boys passed the sacrament tray down the row of pews, alternating back and forth until the sacrament made its way to us. My dad skipped partaking as part of his repentance plan, no doubt. Withholding a broken piece of stale bread and a piddly sip of water for a few months hardly seemed like any sort of punishment at all. I had had a similar sentence for previous transgressions, like admitting to swearing or having impure thoughts. My mom dutifully took hers, then would bow her head in what seemed like pleading with the powers that be.

'Please,' she must have thought. 'Please make this nightmare end.' Some days I took mine, some days I didn't. But while everyone around me seemed to engage in some sort of lowered gaze, thoughtful prayer, I stared straight ahead at the hypocrites on the pulpit.

Sitting up there, watching and judging us in the congregation, mentally taking note of who was or wasn't taking the sacrament. The feelings of trust and respect I had once had for them were long gone. The years of naively, innocently singing songs about popcorn popping on apricot trees seemed wasted, lost. Years of promises I had made of living standards of righteousness as a child of God— where was He when I needed him most? The church leaders were His mouthpiece, His spokesmen. If what they had said was the Word of God, then I felt abandoned and unloved by Him.

I hated them for what they had told my mom. And I hated that my mom felt forced to keep us in the house with my dad. I couldn't help but wonder: if they were keeping my dad's secrets, what *other* secrets were they keeping and for whom? They were the supposed shepherds of our flock, only now I knew they were sheltering wolves among us. My mom must have felt the same way.

She tried; she really did try to keep the faith. Her own mom, my Grandma Libby, had been a convert to the Mormon church, and when she had joined, she did so zealously. I knew my mom wanted to make her proud, to believe what she believed. But, like me, she couldn't justify that the shithole her life had become was what God had in store for her. Finally, she couldn't take it anymore. The chocolate-colored split-level home on Cimarron Lane was sold and our now-fatherless broken family of five moved into a single-wide trailer. At last, I felt like I could sleep at night.

Once the news of my parents' divorce spread, everything changed. My mom became the target of neighborhood gossip, especially among the Filipino families. A few of the wives tsk-tsked her for leaving my dad, telling her that it was their culture to stay with their husbands, no matter what they did. I remembered when we had tried to help our friend Jane, whose father had tried strangling her with her mother's bra she had worn accidentally to school, mistaking it for her own. Our interference with their family business had caused an outrage, and we learned to step back from what we knew was the Filipino way.

My belief in the teachings of our church was fractured beyond repair and with it some of my most treasured friendships. The rest of our Mormon friends had parents who were together, families that were forever, and testimonies that ran deeper and stronger than any earthly friendship. A rift grew between us and I watched helplessly as our paths turned away into infinitely opposite directions. I felt like I was no longer a child of my father's, a child of our congregation, and maybe no longer a child of God.

My mom started nursing school and Christy and I stepped in to help with our younger brothers, dropping them off and picking them up from daycare before and after school every day. One day, shortly after I turned fifteen, as my mom and I drove along just the two of us in the minivan she had bought with our dad, she casually announced that she was thinking of getting back together with him. I immediately bristled at her words. "Why the hell would you do that?" I asked through clenched teeth.

"Something happened," she said, "and it's either a sign from heaven or a sign from hell."

"Are you pregnant?" I asked incredulously. I looked at her, her hands gripping tightly on the steering wheel. She nodded silently, ashamed. My father, she explained, had come to the trailer one night, crying to my mom that he was being shipped off to the Middle East for Operation Desert Storm. He manipulated her into one last night of sympathy sex. And then he didn't even get deployed.

"You're already raising four of us on your own," I logically pointed out. "What's one more? But just know that if you get back together with him, I'm leaving. And this baby better be a girl." (Whaaat? I already had two brothers.)

In October, she delivered my baby sister Jody, and our family of six was complete and sharing the cramped quarters of the single-wide trailer. This baby girl would never live in a house with her dad; she would never know his laugh or the sound of his voice on the rare occasions he raised it; she would never eat the traditional Filipino dish pancit that he made, sometimes with bits of hot dog sliced into it. Her memories of dad would be almost non-existent, as his attempts at fatherhood became feebler. As she got older though, she at least got the expensive purses and wallets too. He later remarried and even had another son, a sibling that none of us would ever know. The idea of having a dad for myself and a grandfather for my kids became alien. Both of my younger boys have asked about him on different occasions, confused that I have a dad (how did they think I was conceived??) and that they had no idea who he was.

I never got any sort of closure with my dad. I don't even know how that would have looked. An "I'm Sorry for All the Years I Snuck into Your Room and Fondled You" card? "Sorry About Your Daddy Issues" postcard? When I was in my late thirties, he sent me a friend request on Facebook. I marinated on it for a few days before accepting, figuring that might be the only way he would ever see his grandkids. Plus, since he was my dad, I felt a weird sense of obligation. It seemed highly unusual to me that he in no other way tried to connect with me or have a relationship with my family. From time to time, he would share one of my posts on his profile, as if to tell the world he was proud of this child of his. Each time he did it, resentment sparked in my chest.

In the fall of 2017, a friend shared on social media about her recent experience at a retreat for sexual abuse survivors. I checked out the link and thought, 'What the hell. I'll apply to attend.' I had started speaking more openly about my past and figured the retreat would offer some valuable insight and information that I could use for my presentations. I quietly submitted my application in October and a couple months later was informed I would be attending in March. I hesitated to tell Dusty for a while, worried about telling him I'd be leaving for five days to go work on this "thing." When I finally got the nerve to tell him, he seemed genuinely surprised.

"What's the retreat for?" he asked.

"For survivors of sexual abuse," I quietly answered.

He slowly nodded. "I've always wondered why you've never really talked about it before."

I wasn't sure how to begin explaining the shroud of silence I had built around my abuse. At that point in time, Dusty and I had been together for nine years and while he knew that I had a *history* of abuse, that was the extent of any conversation we had ever had about it. It's a hard topic to circle back to when you've gotten comfortable and somewhat complacent in a relationship. We were so busy with the grind of everyday life that there never seemed an appropriate time for the talk. Like, "Hey, next time you're at the store will you grab toilet paper? And did I ever tell you about the first time I woke up in pure terror to my dad's unexplained presence in my room? Oh, and we also need more aluminum foil."

I also knew that the healing process of revisiting the past took an emotional toll on me that translated to our own intimacy. I realized that, in the past, I had used sex as a sort of weapon; now I needed to completely change my thoughts and emotions around sex. I'd occasionally tried to work up the nerve to explain these things to Dusty, but every time, the words caught unspoken in the back of my throat. He never asked me specific questions about my past and I never voluntarily offered up any answers. Because if I had learned anything from my experience over the years, it was that past abuse was best left unspoken.

My time at the retreat was invaluable. There were almost thirty women from all over the world, from diverse cultural backgrounds, ages and ethnicities, all there under the common denominator of surviving childhood sexual abuse. We attended workshops, did yoga and Muay Thai, had group and individual therapy sessions, and did therapeutic art projects like *kintsugi*. Healthy, delicious meals were prepared by attentive staff. I felt like an A-list celebrity at a five-star luxury resort in the downtime when I wasn't facing the painful reality of why I and all the other women were there.

I was grouped with six other women over the course of the four days. On our second day at the retreat we had our first group therapy session. Talk about a perfect setting for the things we don't talk about. That first two-hour session dragged on, gaping periods of silence, as each of the women hesitated in sharing any of the horrors of their pasts. By the second session, the conversation flowed a little better, but even then, some of the women stayed completely quiet. In a room of diverse women whose common thread was survivorship, shame still managed to silence us.

Some of us spoke about our abusers: neighbors, uncles, stepdads, brothers, grandfathers, mothers, and fathers. One woman nearly choked as she tried to vocalize the atrocities of being raped by her own husband. Having gone through similar experiences in previous relationships, I knew all too well the feelings of being violated by someone who's vowed to love, honor and cherish you. Shame spewed out and swirled around us; I felt my own mix with others' and wrap around me, warm and comforting. I shared my adoption story; two women shared their abortion stories. One of them looked at me, apologetically.

I explained that I am pro-choice and I am grateful I had the choice to make a decision I could live with. That I would never judge another woman for making whatever choice she could also live with. People assumed since I was a birth mom, I was a pro-lifer. I am, and I believe life is sacred. But sometimes the sacred life *is* that of the mother. If a fifteen-year-old girl was raped and got pregnant, who was I or anyone else to devalue *her* life by making her carry a physical manifestation of sexual assault? There was trauma, grief and shame in either choice, and mine wasn't any better than theirs just because we chose different roads. So many polarized opinions wanted to make an issue black or white when there were layers of gray that clouded the topic.

At the end of the retreat, we wrote anonymous letters to future attendees and received one from a past attendee. The one I got read:

"You are amazing. You are beautiful. You have strength you haven't maybe found yet. I love you. **Write your own story from your truth.** Breathe in and love yourself."

I had started (and stopped and started again) writing this book nearly a year earlier and reading those words made me feel like I was on the right path. The woman who wrote that note had no idea who it would go to or how much I needed that message. It was completely random and sheer serendipity that this specific note would find its way into my hands. Today it is taped to my mirror as a daily reminder of what I am here to do.

I hadn't realized until the time I got to spend at the retreat doing some serious soul-searching, just how much healing I still had in my journey. All the years of silence, of being told or made to feel like I couldn't talk about my abuse, had wreaked major havoc on me. I didn't learn this until I started reading books like *The Body Keeps the Score* by Bessel Van Der Kolk and pretty much anything by Brené Brown. In *Braving the Wilderness,* she wrote:

"Shame thrives on secret keeping, and when it comes to secrets, there's some serious science behind the twelve-step program saying, 'You're only as sick as your secrets.' In a pioneering study, psychologist and University of Texas professor James Pennebaker and his colleagues studied what happened when trauma survivors–specifically rape and incest survivors–kept their experiences secret. The research team found that *the act of not discussing a traumatic event or confiding it to another person could be more damaging than the actual event.* Conversely, when people shared their stories and experiences, their physical health improved, their doctor's visits decreased, and they showed significant decreases in their stress hormones."

Not talking about my dad and the abuse immortalized him and made him, in memories, powerful over me. I did not give permission to my dad to have this power in my life. I still allowed him to have some sort of *control* over me. My silence served as a protection for him and as punishment for me. As soon as I left the remote cabin where the retreat was held and I got into an area with cell phone service, I pulled my car over in a parking lot. My hands shook as I opened my Facebook app and typed in his name. I clicked on the "Unfriend" button. Immediately, a wave of relief coursed through my body.

And then I did what any sane, rational person would do: I started to openly share my story and speak out against sexual abuse as much as possible. I never went into great detail about the abuse itself, other than to say something like, "I am a survivor of childhood sexual abuse" or "I am a one in four" (the statistic of girls in Utah who will be sexually abused before their eighteenth birthday). Still, those words alone sent some audience members searching for the nearest exit. In my presentations, I made it a point to share a quote from one of my favorite books, *The Body Keeps the Score*:

"Nobody wants to remember trauma. In that regard society is no different from the victim themselves. We all want to live in a world that is safe, manageable, and predictable, and victims remind us that this is not always the case. In order to understand trauma, we have to **overcome our natural resistance** to confront that reality and **cultivate the courage** to listen to the testimonies of survivors."

In September of 2018, I flew to Dallas, TX to speak at a women's conference in Southlake. I had researched the area and I knew it was a wealthy, upscale part of the state. Armed with a suitcase full of secondhand clothes and my Kate Spade wristlet, I hoped the women didn't possess the X-ray vision to see that my clothes weren't name brand. I checked into my Air BnB, which I had booked since it was significantly cheaper than the discounted hotel rate offered to the conference attendees. The event organizers sent an email to me and the other speakers, inviting us to go for drinks and appetizers at a nearby restaurant. Eager to start connecting, I headed over from my place in Grapevine, about a fifteen-minute drive.

Y'all, this place was no Applebee's. The minute I walked in and heard the sounds of the live pianist, I felt like my Target dress and strappy sandals may as well have been a burlap sack and bread bags, respectively. I worried what the event organizers would think of me, hell I worried that the hostesses would see what a fraud I was, and that I had no business being there. But I had my Kate Spade wallet that dangled casually from my wrist.

As we were seated at a booth tucked away by the kitchen entrance, Courtney, a soft-spoken woman, remarked, "Oh, what a cute wallet." Back at home I had an adorable wallet with a picture of Frida Kahlo on it that I cherished, but that night at that restaurant where the server offered us a variety of fruits and citruses to add to our purified water, I was grateful to have my Kate Spade wristlet.

From an outsider's perspective it may appear to be a status symbol, a sign of some financial significance. I graciously accept compliments on it, smiling and thinking to myself, "If you only knew." For me, it serves as a shield, protecting the little girl I was, who was forced to carry the burden of shame for decades, who was told not to talk about it. The purse gives me the power that was taken from me as a teenager. It is the symbol of the warrior I am today, no longer silent, no longer ashamed. The purse gives me permission to speak, to heal from trauma, and to courageously share my voice.

I thought that I was the brave one, finally dropping the shroud of secrecy and shame around my abuse and giving voice to the trauma. But my audiences have been brave too, whether they were ready to be or not. And I like to think, like a drop in a bucket, I have helped create a ripple effect to help them become a little more courageous in their own lives as well.

In May of 2018, I spoke at a fundraiser for my local Children's Justice Center, which serves abused kids and is a place "Where Small Voices Can Be Heard." A few months later, the office manager called to tell me that an attendee from that event had reached out to let her know that after hearing my story, they found the courage to get therapy for the damage from their own abusive past.

Hearing this type of feedback always brings me so much joy, knowing that someone else is able to work on their own healing and subsequent personal growth. But this phone call was even more meaningful because it was the first time the feedback came from a man. If I know nothing else, as a woman, about the stigma associated with being a sexual abuse survivor, it is that the stigma is far worse for men. I applaud any male survivor who has the courage to share their story. And those who are not quite ready, I encourage you to find a trusted friend, family member or therapist for when you are.

If you are healing from past sexual abuse, I highly encourage you to find resources near you. You are not alone. You are not at fault. And you have more power than you may think. I see you and I believe you.

For more information about the retreat I attended, go to https://youniquefoundation.org/the-haven-retreat/ and to read some amazing stories from other survivors, check out www.instagram.com/facesofsurvivors.

CHAPTER FIVE:
AUTISM
(BEING THE WEIRDO'S MOM)

**"In an ideal world the scientist should find a method to
prevent the most severe forms of autism but allow the milder
forms to survive. After all, the really social people did not invent
the first stone spear. It was probably invented by an Aspie who
chipped away at rocks while the other people socialized around
the campfire. Without autism traits we might still be living in
caves."**
**~Temple Grandin, American professor of animal science at
Colorado State University, consultant to the livestock industry
on animal behavior, and autism spokesperson**

When my brother-in-law was in college, he had an assignment in
which he had to do something socially unacceptable and then
summarize the reactions of the people around him. He opted to drive
down the interstate in the fast lane, doing twenty miles below the
speed limit. He reported that most of the other drivers responded
with swearing, flipping him the bird, honking, and a general
incredulity of "What the Fuckery."

Sometimes that's what life with an autistic child feels like. We
putter along, doing our thing in our own lane and at our own pace,
while others fly by, judging what must appear to them as our inept
idiocy. They get angry, impatient and annoyed as they hurriedly pass
by, completely oblivious to the greatness of the occupant within.
Sometimes I find myself feeling the same frustrations, both from the
outside looking in and the inside looking out. Autism is an adventure
but sometimes the adventure sucks.

I loved the show "Parenthood." Anybody else? I mean, seriously;
if you haven't watched it, you may need to put the bookmark right

here and proceed immediately to Netflix to binge-watch ALL the episodes. To give you a quick overview, the series was about, well, parenthood. Familial relationships, dynamics, the ups and downs and heartbreaks and achievements. It was truly a magnificent show, even more so for me as an autism mama, since one of the characters on the show, Max, is autistic.

More recently, Netflix produced a show called "Atypical" which I may end up using as a sort of How-To Manual when my own son gets to his late teenage years. While I don't want you to stop reading my highly entertaining book to watch all these Netflix shows, I do encourage you to check them out sometime. Soon. Like right after you're finished reading this. You'll thank me later. But first: finish this. Oh, and don't waste your time on "The Good Doctor." That dude does NOT play a good autistic person. #mytwocents

My only beef with "Parenthood" was when Max's parents received the news of his diagnosis. In the episode, they were DEVASTATED, as if the doctor had said, "Max has leukemia" or "Max has an inoperable brain tumor." You know: a death sentence. That was the level of their reaction to finding out their odd child had autism. And I know, everyone handles things differently, and I don't want to discredit how upsetting it can be to get that kind of news about your child. But autism... autism isn't the end of the world.

I guess for me and our situation it was more of a relief and an oh-yeah-that-totally-makes-sense kind of feeling when Haiden was diagnosed. He had so many of the typical autism traits for so long that it didn't come as a shock to us when, after much testing and observations, the final results were in: Autism Spectrum Disorder, ADHD, and Unspecified Anxiety Disorder. Knowledge was power and knowing what we were up against helped us to prepare for what would be an ongoing battle.

My pregnancy with Haiden was fairly unremarkable, but later, after he was diagnosed, I worried about the glasses of wine I drank before I found out I was pregnant, and then the thousands of Tums I chewed during my second trimester when I was nauseous as hell and trying to get through my double shifts at Red Lobster. I wondered if one or both of these offenses later attributed to my son's diagnosis. Did I have him immunized? Yes. Do I think that's what caused it? No, I do not. Am I sad that me and Jenny McCarthy will probably never be friends because of this debate? Nah, not really.

When Haiden was almost three, his father and I noticed he was developmentally delayed. His speech was practically non-existent and his motor skills weren't age appropriate. Little red flags started popping up in my brain. I don't think I immediately concluded it was autism, but my mommy instincts knew something wasn't right. His pediatrician informed us that it wasn't uncommon for boys to develop slower than girls, so we held off on any sort of official testing for a couple more years.

In the meantime, my marriage to Haiden's dad began to deteriorate. In retrospect, I wondered if some of the stress associated with our son could have contributed to the divorce. There were certainly other issues we had but worrying about a special needs child can put a strain on any marriage or relationship. I researched a little and found conflicting studies that both supported and denied a higher rate of divorce among couples of ASD kiddos. In any case, I ended up a single mom to this boy and learned quickly that I had no clue what I was doing.

Some of the most common traits displayed by ASD people include echolalia, stimming, sensory issues, and obsessions over a particular object, movie, game, etc. Google became my best friend as I started researching all of these topics in hopes of helping my son who I felt was otherwise unreachable. And for the record, these traits are weird, silly, annoying, somewhat socially unacceptable, and sometimes downright hilarious. For example: Echolalia is "meaningless repetition of another person's spoken words as a symptom of psychiatric disorder." Sometimes I would ask Haiden a question and his reply would be whatever the last word I said was, over and over and over like a skipping record. It was as if he loved the feel of the word in his mouth so much he had to keep it there, repeatedly savoring the sensation of it on his tongue. See? Annoying. But also funny.

His stimming over the years has included things like: flapping his hand, sometimes both, so quickly that he looked like he was preparing to take flight; vigorous rocking; the "triple sniff" (exactly what it sounds like- he sniffed three times in succession, over and over); the Violent Cough (I had to email his teachers letting them know that he wasn't sick or dying of tuberculosis); and most recently what I have lovingly come to refer as "The Baby Elephant" wherein he purses his lips tightly together and puffs out a squeak of air. He says he can't stop because his gums are itchy and the squeaking helps. Y'all- I can't make this shit up. We have a veritable Fun House going on over here ALL the time. These stims come and go. Usually he displays one at a time, but every now and then two or more will manifest during the same time period. Sometimes, just to keep it interesting, he throws a new one into the mix; sometimes he recycles an oldie but a goodie. We never know what we're going to get when, but we roll with whatever it is.

The same day we celebrated Haiden's 12th birthday on July 19th, 2017, a fourteen-year-old boy in Arizona was walking through a park when a police officer noticed him behaving strangely. When the officer approached him and asked what the boy was doing with his hands, the boy matter-of-factly replied, "Stimming." The officer, unfamiliar with the term and assuming the boy was on drugs, tackled him to the ground as the boy yelled "I'm okay, I'm okay" and shrieked in terror. The entire incident was captured on the officer's bodycam and aired on the news when the boy's mother, filled with understandable outrage and mama bear heartbreak, insisted that the police get training on how to recognize and appropriately handle autistic people. The news clip I watched showed the teary-eyed mom being interviewed. Her son, seeing her tears, innocently asked, "Are you crying?"

When I came across this news story, I immediately empathized with everything this mom was going through. Having an autistic child, especially a high-functioning one, puts a huge target on their backs everywhere they go. They "look normal" but act weird, suspicious, or like they're on drugs. They lack social skills to understand certain things, like why a police officer might throw them on the ground and shove his knee into their back. I fear almost daily that my son's lack of a filter is going to get his ass kicked, and that the ass-kicking could just as easily come from a cop as it could a bully.

One evening my husband and I had taken our two boys to a basketball game at our alma mater. I was super stoked because I had gotten us amazing seats for free since I served on the board of directors of the alumni association. We were treated to a pre-game dinner of tacos and won some awesome raffle prizes. Aside from a mini-meltdown because there was only ground beef and not chicken for the tacos, all went well until we headed into the basketball arena.

As the announcer's voice boomed into the halls, Haiden abruptly stopped, placed his hands over his ears and yelled, "IT'S TOO LOUD. I CAN'T GO IN."

I attempted to coerce him in. Maybe if you cover your ears with your hoodie that will help, I pleaded. He wasn't having it. He said it felt like bullets were "ricocheting in his brain." That vivid description hurt my heart to think what was so innocuous to the rest of us was so painful for him. My husband suggested leaving him in the lobby with his Minecraft book while the rest of us went in and watched some of the game. I looked around and, seeing two police officers nearby, watching Haiden as he anxiously paced, I told him no, he and Eli could go in without us. I wasn't worried about leaving Haiden alone; I was worried about leaving him alone *around them*.

As far as the spectrum goes, I guess you could say we were lucky to be on the "high functioning" end of things. I have friends whose kiddos are non-verbal, on the "lower end" of the spectrum. I can't imagine not being able to talk to Haiden, even though most of our conversations are ninety percent him talking about something I completely don't understand (Minecraft, Nerf guns, Fortnite, LEGOs??) while I nod and occasionally say, "Mmmhmm." But don't misinterpret his placement on the spectrum to mean that it's all rainbows and butterflies; it's not, we just have it a little easier than others.

We deal with unforeseeable bumps in the road all the time. When he was in kindergarten, I was working on my bachelor's degree. Since he was only in half-day kindergarten and I was in class when he got out, I had to arrange for a daycare that could pick him up until I could get him later in the day. The only one I could find was a dingy, rundown place a few blocks from his school. It looked like it was one bug infestation away from being condemned. I always felt uneasy when I picked him up, watched by the group of motley kids. I had major mom guilt about taking him there, but unfortunately my options were slim.

One day as I dropped him to school his teacher asked me who would be picking him up that day. Confused, I asked her what she meant. The day before, the van driver who always picked him up had told her the daycare was closing immediately. No one from the daycare had said a thing to me, and my stress level shot through the roof of my PT Cruiser as I sobbed on the way to my classes. I scrambled frantically and was extremely fortunate to find an awesome lady who ran a small daycare out of her home which just happened to be right across the street from Haiden's school. Seriously, she was an angel. So was Haiden's teacher, who walked him over there every afternoon. It was a serendipitous blessing in disguise that the dilapidated daycare closed.

In third grade, Haiden had his first experience with a bad teacher, an old, wispy man with spectacles perched precariously on the bridge of his nose and a dry, monotone voice. Secretly, we called him "Mr. Mean". Now normally I try to be a generally nice person who doesn't name-call, but this particular guy I could have called a lot of worse things than that. He had very little patience and tolerance for Haiden, and he made no effort to hide it.

At the beginning of the school year I had brought Mr. Mean a highly informational, personally highlighted article about autism as a resource for him in dealing with Haiden. Two weeks into the school year he admitted to me that he had left it sitting on top of his toilet, unread. On the list of things you shouldn't say to an autism mama, this ranked pretty damn high. I dreaded every day of that school year, feeling like I was sending my kid into the lion's den. The silver lining was that, in an effort to help Haiden succeed, we started having him work with a neurobehavioral psychologist and an occupational therapist. These measures helped, but it was like another full-time job for me, shuttling him to and from appointments every week, sometimes with over two hours of drive time.

I knew that when he started junior high, we would deal with even more adventures but there was no way to adequately prepare ourselves for what would come. During back-to-school night, we walked down the hallways lined with rows and rows of colorfully painted lockers. I never knew that something like this would strike such panic and anxiety in my mama bear heart. When I was in middle school, they were some of the best years of my life. My biggest worries were how many Pound Puppies I could collect, or how big I could tease my bangs for my school pictures. I played clarinet in the band, ate French fries almost every day, and folded notes into tiny origami projects before passing them off to friends in the hallway between classes. I was smart, somewhat popular, and had a bunch of friends.

When Haiden started junior high in 2017, I knew his experience would be *nothing* like mine. For months I dreaded the first day of school. I had mini panic attacks, thinking HOW the hell he would navigate going from class to class, bumping his way through the crowded halls of rowdy kids, and having multiple teachers who needed to learn his idiosyncrasies. What if he got lost? Would anyone help him? What if he had a meltdown? Would kids make fun of him?

He had been a bit of a celebrity at his old elementary school. Teachers loved him and he had a solid group of friends that shared his obsessive interest in Minecraft and LEGOS. At his sixth-grade graduation, my heart nearly exploded when I heard the cheers from his classmates when his name was announced. But heading into junior high, he no longer had one (loving) teacher for the entire day. And district boundary lines had all his bros headed to a different school.

Toward the end of summer, we had to register him at the new school. There was a sort of assembly line set-up: start in this classroom, go to the next, go to the next, etc. We hadn't even made it out of the first room without him breaking into tears. He had to log in to his online profile with the school district. He tried accessing a Google drive from the prior school year and was heartbroken to find that he could not. He openly wailed in the room full of students and their parents, as they stared at us blankly, giving us "The Look."

At twelve years old, my kid had ten pounds and two inches on me. He was a big kid with a loud voice and thick, dark, unruly hair. I realized how this must have looked to the un-autism-acclimated eye. I had gotten "The Look" for years, sometimes mixed with sympathy, maybe even an ounce of understanding. But it was "The Look" nonetheless.

The week before classes started, we had a back-to-school night where we met all the teachers. I stood by nervously as each one introduced themselves to my son. Did they know he was autistic? Was I supposed to tell them? Could they tell on their own? We also got the combination to the locker assigned to him. I knew there was no way in hell he would be able to work the lock. I had him attempt it anyway, hoping maybe I was wrong and he wouldn't have any problem. The school had a "No Backpack" policy, so it was crucial that we figured out the locker.

He turned the dial to each number, then tried to lift the latch.

Nothing. I tried once. Then again. Still couldn't get the damn thing to budge. If I couldn't get the locker open, he *definitely* wouldn't be able to do it. He quickly became frustrated. To diffuse the outburst I could see bubbling up, I told him we'd just have to figure out something else. The school may not have allowed backpacks, but there was no rule against a giant binder… with a strap. Besides, give him a break. He's *autistic.* I don't necessarily like being the parent who thinks my kid is above the rules, but sometimes no matter how hard we tried, we couldn't make all the rules stick for him.

Halfway through the school year, and he still hadn't made any good friends. Kids "used inappropriate language" and "they said Minecraft is overrated, which is dumb because their graphics have had a major overhaul," he told me. Ironically, the class he struggled in the most was his social skills class- a class with other autistic kids. His teacher explained that there were two boys that clashed with our son. They were like water and oil, to which Haiden replied, "And I'm the oil because I'm highly flammable." Seriously. He said this. And it was hilarious. I'm certainly not clever enough to make this up.

One day at lunch, he dropped his sugar cookie on the floor. He asked the lunch ladies for a new one and they refused (don't even get me started on this assholery). In a disappointed rage, he dumped his lunch in the trash, sat down against a wall, and cried. *Could no one have given him a damn cookie??*

I had been inside the school on a few other occasions. And each time, those lockers taunted me, mocking me for the "limitations" of my son. A seventh grader who read on an eleventh-grade level; a kid whose mind was so beautiful, but no one would know because no one would try. A kid who tried so hard to make the numbers work, and *just couldn't get the damn locker door to open.*

In 2016 we started ABA (Applied Behavioral Analysis) therapy, where a therapist (think: the hot girl from Parenthood who came to Max's house and then had to quit because she slept with his uncle, played perfectly by Dax Shepard) would come to our house twice a week for two hours and work on social skills, life skills, behavioral issues, and things like that. Basically, the stuff you don't think about teaching kids because it comes naturally to your "normal" kids is the exact stuff he had to learn how to do. We were very fortunate because my hubby's company offered great insurance that allowed us this much-needed service that so many other special needs families couldn't otherwise afford.

And then, about a year into the therapy sessions, our insurance started denying coverage, citing their policy that they only covered services until the child was nine. We called bullshit and fought back. A child doesn't stop being autistic at nine—it boggled my mind that that was their arbitrary policy. He had been eleven when we started the therapy. We wrote letters, his pediatrician wrote a letter, his teachers wrote letters, all appealing the necessity of the skills he learned in his sessions. After a couple months and a ton of stress and worry, we were elated to hear that the insurance company accepted our appeal and Haiden would be eligible for ABA *indefinitely*.

Ironically, some of the parenting struggles that came as a surprise weren't from atypical Haiden, but the side effects of his autism on our neurotypical kids. I always knew that Haiden would need special treatment, accommodations, and extra attention; I didn't think about how it would impact my older daughter and younger son. When their insecurities started manifesting, I was heartbroken to realize that they felt the way they did. One day, my daughter Mia quietly remarked that all my social media posts were about Haiden. Eli once cried that I loved Haiden more than I loved him. He also started acting out all the time, pushing my buttons and driving me absolutely crazy. After many, many calming breaths it dawned on me that he was really starved for attention, having such stiff competition with Haiden as a brother. The mom guilt of balancing the needs of differently-abled kids was heavier than I ever would have anticipated.

I'm no parenting expert but I did what I thought was the best way to parent without screwing all my kids up too much. We tried to be very open with them, explaining to Eli that yes, it may have seemed unfair that Haiden "gets away" with certain things, but being autistic means he gets a different set of rules. I could tell Eli had thought about this considerably because one day he asked, "Will Haiden *always* have autism?" Yes, I replied. "Will I ever have autism?" I chuckled. Sorry, kiddo— no such luck. But I appreciated his creative thinking. Conversely, Haiden once asked out of the blue if Eli was autistic. When I told him that he wasn't, Haiden replied, "Well then why does he do naughty things, like always talking about his butt?"

Because Haiden tended to be short on patience, I was often caught playing referee between my two boys, and sometimes my older daughter too. When she was pregnant with her first baby and her hubby was deployed, she lived in our basement. On several very unfortunate occasions, she put leftover food in the fridge and Haiden ate it. After the fourth offense, she. lost. her. shit. Lost it. She screamed, swore, and ugly-cried for a good hour. Meanwhile, Haiden was oblivious to her hormonally heightened pregnancy woes and became defensive and obstinate, spiraling into his self-deprecating talk. He wasn't equipped to deal with another person's emotional outburst, so logically he was the worst person in the world and should probably just die. I had to talk both him and Mia off the ledge that day.

The dynamic of parenting a special needs child is hard on marriage too. Dusty is Eli's dad and Mia's and Haiden's stepdad. There aren't too many things we butt heads about, but over the years, how we discipline Haiden has been one of those things. I am the Mama Bear who will protect my cubs, even if it's against Papa Bear. Haiden, who had come a long way over the years, used to really struggle with sudden, unannounced change; if he was doing something he enjoyed and someone said he had to immediately stop without giving him any sort of prior warning, he would meltdown. I worked tirelessly with therapists on strategies to minimize the meltdowns, giving him prompts and warnings so he could prepare to stop his preferred activity when the time came. Dusty would come in like a bull in a china shop, telling Haiden he had to immediately listen and obey. Haiden, quite literally mentally uncapable of performing Dusty's demands, would cry, yell and resist. Dusty saw this as defiance. I saw it as poor parenting. Arguing typically ensued.

Our autism adventure has taught me so much about myself as a person, as a parent, and as an observer and participant in society and the world. I have learned to advocate. I have learned patience beyond measure. I was never much of a spanker anyway, but the one time I lost my cool and popped Haiden on the butt when he was seven, his innocent brown eyes filled with tears and he sobbed, "Why would you do that? Only bullies hit." I felt like the biggest asshole parent. I knew his behavior was not him purposefully acting out, it was the only way he knew how to react in a world that was overwhelming and overstimulating. I could not punish him for that, and certainly I couldn't spank him. I realized that from an outsider's perspective, it might have appeared that he was undisciplined, spoiled, or coddled. But I knew better; and if there was nothing else I had learned over the years of autism parenting, it was that other people's opinions about it were of no consequence to me.

One of Haiden's funniest quirks was his food preferences. He cycled through different foods the way seasons cycle through the year. He's not a picky eater per se; in fact, when he loves a food, he will eat it for every meal or at least eat it every day. His breakfast cycles have included: toaster strudels, cinnamon toast waffles, and extra fluffy double chocolate chip waffles, without syrup. We have gone through the chips and salsa phase when, like clockwork, he would eat those every day as his after-school snack. His most recent craving was chicken taquitos—he'd heat up four in the microwave and then slather them in guac and Frank's hot sauce. He has literally had days where that's all he's eaten. But, as with all his previous foods, once his arbitrary timeline is up, he'll be done with that food and on to the next.

Autism has taught me to have a thick skin. We affectionately called Haiden "Our Little Weirdo" (although at fourteen he was taller than me by six inches and outweighed me by about forty pounds, so he wasn't so little anymore). When he was in pre-school and just starting to become more verbal, I picked him up one afternoon from his usual spot on the playground, in a corner by himself. As I walked toward him a little boy yelled, "Is that your kid?" When I nodded, he nonchalantly said, "He's weird."

I couldn't stop the pang in my heart and the tears that stung my eyes. I glanced at Haiden, worried that he had heard the boy. If he had, he hadn't seemed to notice or care. I realized that this wasn't going to be an isolated incident, this life of being called names. I also knew I couldn't protect him from this or other future asshole kids. So, I decided to prepare him. Yes, I told him, you're a weirdo, but we're all a little weird and there's nothing wrong with that. Using it as a term of endearment was a way for us to create a positive association from an otherwise negative experience, and one, tiny way we could attempt to make the world a little better for him.

Autism has taught me things about myself that translated into my professional life, like the fact that I am a crisis management champ. Crises included, and were not limited to:

- "OMG the school switched the Tuesday lunch menu and they're not serving the regularly scheduled Mandarin Chicken." (I had to rearrange my work schedule and bring him lunch that day.)

- "I'm feeling lonely. I don't want to go to P.E. It's too loud and I'm not a 'P.E. guy'." (I had to pick him up early that day.)
- The principal called to inform me he shouted out in class and it scared the other kids. (This one the principal handled until I picked him up after school and had to discuss with him why we don't yell just because we're pissed off about Common Core math. I get it, dude—we ALL hate Common Core math.)

I learned to stay calm, to not overreact, and that no matter how stressful it was in the moment, it would pass and we would survive. These instances made every other work stressor pale in comparison. If I could handle regular calls from the principal, I could handle anything. Bring. It. On. Angry customer? No problem. Manager wanted to meet with me before the staff sales meeting to "discuss some things"? I was cool as a cucumber. Years of autism-related shenanigans had prepared me for many, many hard conversations I would have otherwise avoided. That's not to say there weren't tears shed during the actual crises—but after a little time and distance from the calamity, I was able to find the humor and laugh about them.

I learned that I had no control over time but that I could still be productive and successful. I once went to a networking lunch where the speaker, a well-known, wealthy, successful man posted a picture of his daily schedule to explain how he time-blocked his day. He literally had every hour accounted for, including his time with his kids. I was really good about writing out my daily schedule and following my to-do lists, but I also knew that if shit hit the fan and something happened with Haiden (which was not uncommon), I *had* to take care of him first. Autism don't give a damn what else you had planned for the day. Double snap, double snap, sashay. Nuh-uh, honey child.

This happened when I was in classes at college and it happened when I was working. It didn't matter where I was or what I was doing. If I got a call from the school saying I had to come get him, I dropped whatever I had going on and I went to get him. I still managed to graduate Summa Cum Laude as the Outstanding Graduate for my major and win a huge industry award for my work in 2017. I had many days that didn't go exactly according to plan, but

I learned to adjust course like a champ.

Admittedly, not all of the life lessons from raising a special needs child have been positive ones. There were days when I couldn't suppress feelings of bitter jealousy bubbling up when I scrolled through social media and saw post after post of other people's perfect kids. Getting straight As, scoring the winning soccer goal, winning the football game: all things that Haiden would never do. Once, after one of the many, many trips I had to take to his school to help talk him down from an outburst or, if he threw a chair in the library, bring him home, as I pulled out of the school parking lot, I glanced at the marquee. My OB/GYN, the doctor who had delivered Eli, had two accomplished sons, one of whom attended Haiden's school. Her son's name flashed across the screen, a congratulatory proclamation for all of our town to see. I wistfully wondered under what, if any, circumstances I'd ever see Haiden's name lit up like that.

I don't *want* to be jealous of other people's kids' accomplishments. Of *course* they should be proud of their amazing kids and what they're doing. And I have two neurotypical kids who are also doing great things. But yes, sometimes it's hard that Haiden won't have certain experiences in his life. What I've learned is that those are my preconceived notions about how I see my children as an extension of myself. And just because his journey looks extraordinarily different than what mine was or what I had hoped his would be, doesn't mean it's a bad journey.

I've heard people say that giving kids participation awards was stupid and I'd think, were it not for that type of recognition, Haiden would never win *anything*. When he was required to participate in the school's science fair in sixth grade, I wasn't sure we would make it through that hellfire unscathed. On the cover of the composition notebook in which he was supposed to track the results of his project, he angrily scribbled, "I will not write anymore stupid things in this stupid piece of crap." When he finally did, and he won his participation ribbon at the science fair, I couldn't have been prouder, and I snapped a picture of him in front of his school's marquee to commemorate the ordeal.

The weirdest, wackiest shit thus far though has been (gulp) puberty. When he started getting underarm hair and his deodorant got clumped up in it, he got super agitated and had me cut it out.

One year for Eli's *Toy Story* themed birthday, we got a life-size balloon of Buzz Lightyear. A few days later, I walked in and found Haiden, well… let's say he was enjoying him. To infinity. And beyond! In keeping with his love of Disney, he developed a major crush on Judy Hopps, the bunny from *Zootopia*. He could tell you every detail about her, from her height to her middle name to the exact shade of purple of her irises. It was truly sweet how much he adored her. Other kids his age thought it was less "adorable" and more "dumb," and he was ridiculed about it at school.

The biggest heartbreak we battled in junior high was the loss of his three BFFs, the only boys he had regularly hung out with since kindergarten. As they got older, the other boys made new friends and acquired new interests. Haiden no longer seemed to be of any interest to them. Invitations to parties and sleepovers stopped. When we invited any of them over, none of them could come. I tried finding other moms of quirky kids to see if any of them would click with Haiden. But finding friends for autistic kiddos—there isn't an app for that.

Being Haiden's mom is one of my greatest accomplishments. I never set out to become any sort of advocate, but as I've shared our story and become a sort of voice in the ASD community, it has been a natural progression. I have been criticized for it, accused of exploiting him. I am vocal about *many* things (like, duh, tots obvs) because I think it's important to do my part in bringing awareness and acceptance, as well as creating change for future ASD generations. I feel so passionately about it that I created Awesome Autistic Ogden, an autism awareness event/community, as well as a nonprofit called Bernal Badassery Foundation. If I help teach one asshole to be nice to a special needs kid, I can die proud of a life well-lived.

I recently had a fellow autism mom tell me that if she could eliminate or cure her son of autism, she would. I truly had to think about that one. Would I wish for my son to be neurotypical? I don't think I would. He has an amazing mind and is quirky AF. He is legit one of the biggest weirdos I have ever met, and I adore him exactly as he is. I may not be able to make him fit into the world, but I will do my best to make the world fit for him.

CHAPTER SIX:
BREAST IMPLANT ILLNESS
(A TALE OF TWO TITTIES)

"More often than not, the ideal breast is an invented breast. Décolletage, the tushy breast, is an artifact of clothing. Naked breasts don't dance cheek to cheek--they turn away from each other. Breasts vary in size and shape to an outlandish degree, but they can be whipped into an impressive conformity, and because we are human and we can't leave anything alone, we have whipped away."
~Natalie Angier, nonfiction writer and a science journalist for The New York Times

At the beginning of 2008 I was a thirty-one-year-old bartender going through my third divorce. I was struggling in my career as a Realtor during one of the biggest market crashes in recent history, and since that was going somewhat miserably, I fell back on what I had been doing for over ten years and knew how to do well: slingin' beers and entertaining the regulars at the local brewery, Roosters. With my dazzling personality and my lightning fast quick wit, I was a natural.

Faced with the reality of life's bleak outlook, I decided I should celebrate my new singlehood with a pair of perky, round tatas that I absolutely could not afford. I had nursed a couple babies, gone through multiple weight fluctuations, and my titties were a mess. Nobody wanted to see a bartender with un-fun fun bags. And since bartending was going to be my livelihood for the unforeseeable future, a boob job seemed like the perfect investment for a broke, soon-to-be single mom.

In high school, I had been blessed with beautiful B-cup breasts. I remember comparing bra sizes with girlfriends one night at a sleepover, and my flat-chested friend Heidi swore she too was a B-cup. I demanded to see proof. Sighing and rolling her eyes, she unsnapped her bra and slid it out from under her t-shirt, tossing it to me defiantly. I unrolled the little tag to reveal the words "Absolutely A". We exploded in laughter. Even as teenagers, we knew that a certain level of our worth was based on the cup size of those training bras. (Why *are* they called training bras? What exactly were they training for? Or, more accurately, what were they training *us* for?)

I knew I was lucky (#blessed) to have blossomed into my B-sized bosom. Most Filipinas are quite flat-chested, and I am after all, half Filipino. I guess I owed my above-average cuppage to my mom's side of the genetic equation. Still, by the time I was in my thirties, my jibbly bits had seen their fair share of boobie battles. When I nursed, I ballooned to a DD. When I quit nursing and lost weight, they shriveled to Barely Bs. They hung like sad fruit roll-ups from my chest.

I began to loathe them. I didn't want them to be touched. I referred to them as "Puddle Boobs". And there were only so many secrets Victoria's Secret could keep for me. I was being held up by wire, padding, and gel inserts. I hated the feel of underwire, how it would dig into my flesh and leave marks. I wore a water bra— a contraption filled with mini sacs of liquid to emulate the look of implants. I'd hoist them into whatever new, ungodly contraption was on the market, hoping for the fulfillment of the promised miracle. Remember that scene in the wildly popular Bette Midler movie *Beaches*? Like Otto Titsling, I tried everything for my over-the-shoulder-boulder-holders. After years of dealing with my mammary maladies, I finally made an appointment with a plastic surgeon. My mom had gotten a boob job several years prior, and if it was good enough for her, it was good enough for me.

I remember the excitement I felt at the consultation when the doctor pulled out a variety of clear, squishy orbs for me to fondle. He had me "try on" several different sizes, stuffing them into my bra and examining myself in the mirror from every angle. I nearly exploded with the glee I felt when I saw the busty babe looking back at me. I was ready to get sliced open to get them bad boys in as soon as possible. Afterward, he took some pictures and measurements, lifting my flapjack flops and explaining how the incision scar would look from the lift. When the girl at the front desk cheerfully handed me the sheet of paper with the quote for the procedure, I ignored the voice of reason that was loudly shouting in my head not to do it. Carefree as a Kardashian, I paid my deposit and scheduled the surgery.

The procedure I ended up having cost $6500, which I paid for by maxing out a couple credit cards that I would later file under my post-divorce bankruptcy. My boobs were doomed from the get-go. I also ended up three separate times going under the knife. AND the surgeon explained that the life expectancy of the implants was ten years, after which time I'd have to replace them. In my over eagerness I didn't care; I would cross that bridge in ten years. I wanted them NOW and besides, ten years was a long ways away.

First, I had a lift to tighten the sagging skin on the underside of my breasts and lift my nipples from their downward droop. The plastic surgeon made a vertical incision from the underside of my breast up to and around my nipple, which was removed and then reattached. A patch of excess skin was removed before my breast was stitched back together in what is known as a "keyhole" incision. After six weeks of recovery from the lift, I then had the implants placed— generous 400 ccs of Mentor Silicone— under my pectoral muscles. Shortly after implantation, my left breast started leaking blood from the incision around my nipple and I had to go back to the surgeon to have a hematoma drained.

I had gone against doctor's orders about taking it easy and had flown across the country from Utah to South Carolina to spend St. Patrick's Day with my ex-husband/then boyfriend, Stacey. I'm not sure if there's any way to adequately portray the horror of realizing you're bleeding non-stop from your breast, drunk on Red Bull and vodka, surrounded by a bunch of other drunk fools, and you're nearly two thousand miles from home. The next day, I thought I would die on the flight back to Utah, especially when I had to navigate the craziness of the Atlanta airport, doped up on pain meds and hungover as hell. As soon as I landed in Salt Lake City, I went to my plastic surgeon for emergency surgery and had to go under anesthesia and the scalpel again. But once I finally recovered from all that, I was a new woman with my Bionic Breasts! Oh, the places I (and my boobies) would go!

I started running a couple months after getting my implants. Prior,

I had felt that my sad, saggy bits would be too much for a sports bra to support; also, I had no desire to run. Once I started though, I was hooked and I've been a runner ever since. Years before my boob job, I had dated a guy who told me that my breasts in a sports bra looked like a loaf of bread. Picture that— one continuous mound of soft flesh, with no distinct separation. I don't think he meant it as a compliment, much as I love me a loaf of Great Harvest Honey Wheat.

In retrospect, I wonder about the correlation between my new cleavage, which I had even in unflattering, boob-flattening sports bras, and my love of fitness and running. Once, during a Ragnar Relay race, a friend paced me on my last seven-mile run. He glanced over toward my bouncing bosom and proclaimed: "I never noticed how big your...calves are." Mmmhmm. I bet. (Although I do have some nice calves if I say so myself.)

The boobs worked their magic, making me feel better, sexier, and more confident. I enjoyed wearing a bunch of new styles of clothes I couldn't before: tube tops, halter tops, backless, even braless! All my patrons at the brewery loved my new fun bags. I took every opportunity I could to show them off, proud as a new mom to my beautiful twins. The stress of my divorce had also helped me shed a few pounds, so I was skinny and busty all at once. For a hot minute, I felt like an incarnation of Jessica Rabbit.

I even ended up snagging a new husband! Dusty was the loan officer for the last real estate deal I did before calling it quits as a Realtor. (In his defense, he said he didn't fall for me for my boobs. Nor was it my credit score. But in any case, the D-cups certainly helped him overlook what a mess my creditworthiness was when we met to see if he could qualify me for a teeny tiny mortgage. He couldn't.)

But truth be told, I still didn't *love* my breasts. The porn stars with huge, cartoonish globes didn't sport the obvious scars like I had from the lift. And while the placement of the implants created a robust bust on the topside, the bottoms of my breasts still sagged, especially when I leaned over. For all intents and purposes, they were and would always be Franken-boobies. I would never attain the unrealistic societal ideal of the perfectly round jugs.

When I had Eli in June of 2012, I tried nursing him but because my nipples had been completely detached and reattached during the lift, my milk ducts had been severed and I was unable to. I felt horrible and guilty that I couldn't use my breasts for their intended purpose of feeding my child. My hormones hadn't gotten the memo about my non-functioning nips and when my milk came in, I became engorged and it felt like my chest was on fire. It was the first time I felt big regret about my boob job. On top of all that, Eli was jaundiced and had to be strapped into a bilirubin bed for hours at a time. It was a bit traumatic the first couple weeks with the newest addition.

In the summer of 2017, a friend and fellow runner shared in a private Facebook group her decision to have her breast implants removed. She cited a website and a condition called Breast Implant Illness. This piqued my curiosity and I started doing my own research, as I had begun to experience a few unexplained symptoms over the previous year. In September, I consulted with a plastic surgeon and brought up BII. I could tell immediately that he thought I was stupid and/or crazy. My implants, he told me, could theoretically last my lifetime. I was shocked to hear this since I had known since I got them that their "shelf life" was ten years.

I left his office feeling doubtful and dumb. Maybe my mysterious ailments could be attributed to something else. Maybe I was just dealing with age-related issues. I tucked away the papers his nurse had given me and told myself it was all in my head. The months ticked by, and I began to notice symptoms more and more, and remembered issues I had had before and wondered why, as an otherwise healthy woman, they weren't subsiding. Specifically, I had been experiencing:

- Ringing ears
- Brain fog
- Extreme fatigue
- Dizziness/nausea
- Breast pain (and a small lump that had sent me to the doctor for a mammogram)
- Chest pains/shortness of breath
- Weird skin issues on my neck, chin and cheeks
- Low libido (like, ridiculously low)
- Anxiety/depression

Over the course of 2016-2018, I had had a hearing test,

bloodwork, and even a few pregnancy tests to try to determine what the hell was wrong with me. I thought I might have early onset menopause; maybe a thyroid or Vitamin D deficiency. Every test came back normal. I exercised and ate right, yet I could never lose weight and I was exhausted every day. In my runner's mind, I was strong and should be able to do whatever I wanted to do; but more and more it became a huge struggle. Suddenly the fun bags didn't seem so fun.

I had joined an online community of thousands of women who were experiencing some version of symptoms, ailments, and autoimmune diseases. Many of them were deathly ill. In June of 2018 I started training for a Half Ironman. On two separate occasions, I went for a short swim and came out of the water shaking, nauseous, and dizzy as hell. I was scared to drive the winding canyon road home from the lake. How in the world would I be able to swim three times that distance, bike fifty-six miles, and run a half marathon if I felt that sick from a short swim? After the second miserable swim I told my husband it was time to evict the toxic titties.

I consulted with a different plastic surgeon, one who didn't discount the possibility of my implants making me sick. I looked at my calendar, trying to determine a time that wasn't full of major life events. We had a family vacation to Maui scheduled for September and a grandbaby due in October, so I decided the sooner the better and scheduled my explant for Friday the 13th of July. What better day to get sliced open than Friday the 13th? Although I was saddened by the thought of my first trip to Maui and not having the busty bosom along for the ride, I knew the tatas' time had come.

Explanting was not a decision made lightly or blindly; it was well-researched, expensive and inconvenient. It required me to miss out on quite a few races I had signed up for (including my triathlon), time off work and exercising, and valuable summer fun time with my family. But I didn't regret it one bit. My eyes were brighter and significantly less puffy just hours after my procedure. The day after surgery I took a picture of my face and was shocked to see the obvious contrast. The weird cheek acne and dryness around my chin and neck literally was gone. I told my husband I felt like a Disney Princess (although that could have been the Lortab talking). We also learned the valuable lesson that I am not to be trusted with Amazon Prime while on pain meds, when a set of plastic pink flamingos and a flimsy bra resembling a slingshot showed up on our doorstep during my recovery.

I had draining tubes in for ten *miserable* days but once they and my stitches were out, I felt much better. What are 'draining tubes,' you ask? Long, flexible tubes that are placed into the breast and held in by a stitch, with small bulbs attached at the end into which fluid drained. They are meant to help in the healing process and to avoid unfortunate events like the hematoma I had gotten when I got my implants. When I was cleared to shower a couple days after surgery, I clipped the bulbs to a lanyard around my neck. I moved slowly and gingerly, fearing the agony of accidentally tugging too hard on the tubes. Getting the drains removed was relatively quick and painless and a huge relief.

I took four weeks of rest before I slowly started back with my running. That was probably the hardest part for me, especially since I was running a half marathon every month that year. I had timed my July run to be the day before surgery and my August one to be the last day that month. Adjusting to the new tatas was a lot of trial and error. I had to invest in smaller, tighter sports bras that compressed me to the point of looking like a boy to keep my tender jibbly bits from bouncing too much, but also allowed me to breathe. I discovered that the world is a lot bouncier than I had realized. Body Combat? Bouncy AF. Driving through road construction? Ow ow ow ow ow. Working my chest muscles was a very slow comeback since they would spasm if I even thought about doing a push-up. I had no doubt they were fairly traumatized post-surgery, readjusting to the new normal without the ginormous orbs of silicone.

I know that there are those who will argue that there's no scientific evidence to support Breast Implant Illness. As one small, unscientific voice I would just say: There's no scientific evidence *yet.* But after watching the Netflix documentary *The Bleeding Edge* and realizing how easy it is to get a stamp of FDA (U.S. Food and Drug Administration) approval, I wouldn't be surprised to see evidence coming to light in the near future. Apart from that, I know my own relationship with my implants and I was happy to be rid of them. In the year prior to explanting, I had nightmares in which I tried cutting open my chest and pulling them out myself.

When I was a teenager, I went on a hike during my church's summer camp, deep in the woods of South Carolina. Our group ended up getting off course and we were lost for hours. When we were found and rescued (it sounds more dramatic than it was), one girl found a tick that had embedded in her leg. We were instructed to check ourselves to make sure the nasty bloodsuckers hadn't latched on to anyone else. I had showered and done a pretty thorough job of searching and had not found any ticks on my body. Later, after shoveling food into my starving belly at the chow hall, camp leaders instructed us to check each other's hair, particularly the dark-haired girls. One of my friends started parting sections of my long, thick, dark hair and at the nape of my neck found that a tick had indeed burrowed its way under my skin. We were able to get it out intact, but for years afterward, I would wake up from nightmares in which I looked at my hand and, just below the surface of the skin, an army of ticks was squirming around. The horror invoked by that dream was the same way I felt about my implants.

I've had MANY people, both men and women, ask me about my experience. I would tell anyone with implants, both saline and silicone, to research Breast Implant Illness. It seems like more and more women are going through some sort of battle with theirs, some severely sick. I'm glad I didn't get to that point, but I believe it only would have been a matter of time. I don't think I could have been talked out of my decision to get implants when I did, as much as I wish I could; it would have saved me A LOT of money. But I would certainly caution other women against it. It kind of horrifies me to think I was carrying heavy, toxic, unnatural bags so close to my vital organs for so long.

In November 2018, news stories and articles began surfacing about a cancer that was linked to breast implants. Additionally, an investigative team of journalists from around the world compiled an article with some startling statistics about breast implants. In part, the article read:

"For years, the FDA allowed breast implant companies to bury evidence of ruptures and other injuries by reporting them as routine events that did not require public disclosure. When the FDA tightened enforcement of its reporting rules in 2017, reports of injuries soared, and they are on pace to increase more than 20-fold in the last two years from the previous two-year period...

Experts say the surge in reports doesn't mean breast implants have suddenly gone bad; it's that they were never as safe as the data

— and the FDA's approval — implied in the first place… In the U.S. and Canada, regulators did not impose any consequences after manufacturers lost track of most of the participants in a large-population health study within three years, although a 10-year study was ordered as a condition of allowing silicone implants back on the market.

In September 2018, researchers at the MD Anderson Cancer Center in Houston reported the results of the largest-ever long-term safety study of breast implants. The study found associations between silicone implants and three autoimmune diseases. In the same month, an Israeli study of tens of thousands of women also discovered a link between breast implants and autoimmune diseases. Several smaller studies conducted in recent years in the Netherlands and the U.S., reached similar conclusions. The studies did not prove that implants were causing the ailments but showed that women with breast implants were suffering these diseases at statistically significantly higher rates than women without implants."

The full article can be found here: https://www.icij.org/investigations/implant-files/breast-implant-injuries-kept-hidden-as-new-health-threats-surface/?fbclid=IwAR1VguzYsk31qGlOzZz6MvSZl9aghvQeEgVF0_m55V5QXz7zIRY2AwuUa0M

The more I researched, the angrier I got. Angry that I had wasted so much money to get the implants in and subsequently out; angry that these toxic bags hadn't been through rigorous studies before being sewn into millions of women's chests; and angry that I ever felt the societal pressures to look a certain way that I would risk my own health over vanity. Government, implant manufacturers, and most plastic surgeons don't seem to care about the hazards associated with implants. Sadly, many women don't care either. Like tobacco use or any other carcinogenic substance, we're willing to take the risk. There is now a known cancer linked specifically to implants, and as of July 2019, the implant manufacturer Allergan had issued a recall on several of their implants.

I won't lie and say I don't sometimes miss the fake boobies. I am a broad-shouldered woman so having a bust helped create some femininity for my frame. Now, especially in a sports bra, I feel like a pre-pubescent boy. The fact that I chopped my hair to a pixie cut (it was so damn cute, though) didn't help. Fortunately, with a well-padded albeit uncomfortable Victoria's Secret bra, I can still look like I have boobs; unfortunately, the underwire still sucks. Is Victoria a sadist and can't she do any better in the bra department? I wear a lot of bralettes, which do nothing for my silhouette, but they feel oh-so-much better. I am fortunate to have a decent handful of breast tissue (as long as we're measuring by my relatively small hands) and can *almost* create some cleavage with a good cup-and-hoist maneuvering. I just jiggle a little like a flan that hasn't quite set. But who doesn't like flan?

My husband never knew me before my implants, and while he has been supportive along this journey, I'm sure he misses the fun bags. I mean, he certainly enjoyed them when they were around. I joke that he married a busty brunette and now he has a flat-chested redhead. I consider myself lucky, though, because I've heard stories of women whose husbands/boyfriends/partners left them when they decided to explant. I think that's a sad commentary on our culture if fake boobs are that important to men that they would overlook the damage they're doing to women, and they would leave a relationship over them.

Women are not their breasts. In fact, I find myself gently reminding people when they ask me about "getting rid of my boobs" that I did *not* get rid of them. What I got rid of was several pounds of potentially poisonous toxins that were shoved and unnaturally manipulated under my pectoral muscles. And they are, most definitely, NOT my boobs. They're currently residing in a bag in my closet until I think of some more creative use for them. Maybe cornhole? Paper weights?

My biggest post-surgery perk is that, having spent almost eleven years with a set of DDs, I occasionally *feel* like I still have DDs. Either that or else I have become so secure and self-aware that I just don't give a shit anymore about how my breasts look. If I want to wear a spaghetti strap halter dress without a bra, I'll do it. I have quickly adapted and adjusted to a smaller bustline, able to zip up and button certain dresses and shirts that I couldn't before. I have a picture of me at an event in a sequined Wonder Woman corset bustier and I can't fathom how my nibbly bits weren't peeking over the edge of it. I had gotten so used to that voluminous cleavage that when I see it now, I can't imagine how I hauled those bad boys around for as long as I did.

For my own purposes I documented my breast implant removal journey with before and after pictures. On my phone. When I had to register Haiden for eighth grade classes, we showed up at the junior high and had to get through a series of steps in order to finalize enrollment. The first stop had us packed into the sweltering auditorium with lots of other kids and parents, waiting for school pictures and ID cards.

After he took his turn smiling awkwardly for the photographer, we had to sit and wait while the ID card was printed and laminated. Haiden asked for my phone to keep him entertained while we waited. Nonchalantly, I handed it over. I can't fully explain the sheer terror or the level of embarrassment I experienced when, a few minutes later, he loudly burst out, "WHY do you have inappropriate pictures on your phone?!" The already hot auditorium now felt like the fiery pits of hell and I sunk down into the creaky old seat, feeling the stares of the people around us. I briefly considered waving and saying, "Yeah, hi. I'm the slutty mom of the weird autistic kid."

But traumatic moments like this aside, the most valuable takeaway, by far, is the lessons in self-love that I have experienced throughout this tale of two titties. The woman I was when I made the decision to get breast implants was mentally, emotionally and spiritually bankrupt. I was a broken person, having never adequately dealt with the abuse from my past; having made regrettable choices in men and marriages; and having spent most of my life with very low self-esteem. I had very little regard or appreciation for my worth because I felt so very flawed and, for lack of a better summary, worthless. I felt that maybe if my physical body could prove that I had any sort of value, then big boobs must be the answer.

This isn't to imply that I think every woman who opts for a boob job does so from a place of insecurity. There are many reasons for choosing cosmetic plastic surgery, but I feel safe saying there are certainly societal standards that impact this decision. In a photoshopped, social media-obsessed world, we tend to become a product of that which we consume. Anthropologically speaking, big, fake breasts are not a universal trend. That which is considered beautiful is a culturally biased derivative.

A quick Google search shows that the good ol' US of A ranks number one worldwide in cosmetic surgeries. And a 2017 study titled,

"Cosmetic Surgery and Body Image Among Utah Women," co-authored by research fellows Janika Dillion and Robbyn T. Scribner, states that Salt Lake City is second in the nation in plastic surgeons per capita, making it second to Miami and ahead of Los Angeles. "In Utah, 87.6 percent of the population identifies as white, and Utah tops all the states in having the highest population of one religion: 57 percent are Mormon. These factors might be linked to high plastic surgery rates," according to the study. "The study also suggests that growing household incomes and social media might attribute to the pressure. Viewing pornography, where Utah was the first to declare pornography as a public health crisis, is another factor."

The same Google search brings up a 2011 scholarly journal article which states: "In developing countries, aesthetic procedures constitute [a] very small part of plastic surgery interventions and plastic surgery units are primarily required for reconstructive needs for optimum management of patients." In other words, where some countries demand big boobs, small noses, and liposuctioned backsides, others beg for minimal scarring from burns or birth defects.

I don't judge people who choose plastic surgery in an effort to ameliorate their appearance. As a rehabilitated giver of fucks, I feel sympathetic more than anything. We have been fed lies and absurdities about how we should look and what we should do to be more attractive and therefore happier and more successful. It's an "If this then that" mentality. "If I have big boobs, then I will be happy." At what point in time do we stop looking outward for acceptance and approval and become content with who we are? In my own journey of self-acceptance, I became startlingly aware that this vehicle, this physical body that is serving me during my fleeting time on this planet, is *just that*: it's a protective barrier to my heart and soul, the bits that truly make me a good human.

The biggest surprise of this journey is how polarized people are about BII. Whether you believe it or not, it doesn't need to be an all-out war among those with or without implants. When I told people about my experience, I did so purely for informational purposes. I hadn't realized until months after the fact, when one of my former good friends sent me an angry text about a completely different subject and wrote: "Well I still have my 'toxic titties.'" And like the Tag Team song goes, "Whoomp There it Is." That's why (or at least partly why) she was no longer friends with me. I had no idea that along with the breasties I'd lose some besties, and it took a while to recover from the pain of those losses.

I'm not talking about losing some inconsequential acquaintances, either. I'm talking about BFFs, women who were like sisters to me, and with whom I shared a matching tattoo. I noticed shortly after my explant surgery that there was a dynamic shift between us, but it was also less than a month after Kyle had died and I thought that was a big part of it. I had to take almost two months of recovery time, so I figured that had a little to do with my feeling left out. But even once I got back into the groove, there was definite weirdness and tension.

I started getting that feeling like when you walk into a room and everyone stops talking and you think they're talking about you. I realized, when I saw pictures of them on social media, I was purposely excluded from events that we had previously done together. By the end of 2018, the tribe in which I had been encircled for three years had basically cast me out. I felt like I had gone through a bad breakup. I had lost Kyle, my tatas, and some of my best friends.

And it wasn't so much that I had my implants removed; it was that I had the nerve *to openly talk about* having them removed. I was criticized for sharing things on social media and told I should "better" myself quietly. I had already spent my time keeping quiet and had found that it served me no purpose. Many women have reached out to thank me for sharing about BII, and I will never be sorry for helping someone else in their own journey back to health and self-love following breast implant removal.

I think there's a perception that, with personal growth, there comes a sense of betterment. That couldn't be further from my experience. Nothing I have done or will do makes me "better than" anyone else—it's just *different*. My evolution doesn't make me better than anyone; it's not a competition or comparison.

I love my stretch marked belly, the puckered skin around my navel that resembles a butthole more than a belly button. I embrace my deflated, jiggly breasts, especially my left one since it's noticeably bigger than my right; I can be beautifully, perfectly imperfect. I can wear whatever type of bathing suit I feel like flaunting at the water park on hot summer days. I can catch a glimpse of my naked body, tattooed and saggy in spots, and bask in its glory, appreciative for its capacity to run marathons, to swim, to cycle, to dance. I thank my body for having safely brought four beings into this world. I feel genuine gratitude for the things I am able to physically accomplish. And so can you and everyone else. Love your body; thank it every day for all it does for you; and allow others that same joy.

CHAPTER SEVEN:
ADOPTION
(WHO'S THE BABY DADDY?)

"If I could just have the thing and give it you now I totally would, but I'm guessing it looks probably like a sea monkey right now, so we should probably let it get a little cuter, right?"
~ Ellen Page as Juno, *Juno*

In November of 1993, when I was a junior in high school, I found out I was pregnant. I was the drum major of the marching band and the younger sister of the Valedictorian of that year's graduating senior class. I went to a small school in the town of Goose Creek, SC. News of my pregnancy spread faster than a forest fire. Retrospectively, I joked that everyone else knew before even I did. I think the shock value of a Mormon "Band Nerd" getting pregnant added fuel to the flames.

My boyfriend, Stacey, was my high school sweetheart. We had started dating my freshman year when he was a senior. After he graduated, he went to college about two hours away from our hometown. Over the course of the next couple years, we were on again off again—but mostly on. When I found out I was pregnant, we decided fairly quickly the best thing to do was to give the baby up for adoption. But first we needed to tell our parents.

I don't really remember how his parents took it. They were going through their own stuff at the time, as we found out later when they filed for divorce. They didn't get too involved with the messiness of my pregnancy. I was scared to death to tell my mom. A few years prior, she and my dad had gotten divorced. She bought a mobile home for us to live in while she worked full-time and put herself through nursing school. My dad had already rocked her world with his abusive and adulterous scandals, and I hated that I now had another bomb to drop on her.

To prevent my untimely death at the hands of my mother, I decided to tell her one night while we ate fried fish and hush puppies at Captain D's. For added protection, my friend Adam was there too. He wasn't aware of my pregnancy announcement either, so when I finally got the nerve to blurt it out between bites of tartar sauce-covered halibut, his and my mom's expressions of shock were almost comical.

"What makes you think you're pregnant?" my mom asked, panicked.

"Welllll, I took a test. And it was positive."

I let the news sink in as I continued to shovel fried goodness into my mouth. Finally, my mom said something I never expected.

"I'll support you, whatever you decide."

Now it was my turn to be blindsided. Despite my current "unwed mother" state, I had grown up in a somewhat religious household, and always considered myself to be a pro-lifer. In fact, just a couple months before, for an English assignment, I had written an entire paper supporting this belief. I had even gone to a women's clinic to gather information and they had given me a gold-plated pin of a set of two tiny feet, meant to represent the size of a fetus' feet at the time most abortions occur. I proudly wore that pin all the time.

Insulted, I looked my mom right in the eye.

"I'm giving it up for adoption," I stated firmly. "There's nothing else I would do."

She nodded. There was pain and sadness in her eyes, but something like pride, too. She asked me if I'd want to go through the adoption services through our (almost-former) church. I felt strongly against this idea since I harbored resentment from how church leaders had handled my abuse a few years earlier. I didn't want to predispose my child to that same religion. She asked if I'd consider adopting within our family. I had an aunt who had been trying to have another child for years after she had had her son. That felt way too weird to me. When that aunt later got sick and passed away from ALS in 2001, I felt even more grateful about my decision. I couldn't imagine what I would have felt knowing my biological child watched a parent die.

My mom was a labor and delivery nurse at a hospital in Charleston. One night at work, she told a co-worker about my pregnancy predicament. That co-worker mentioned a nurse who worked in post-partum who had been having infertility struggles for a while. My mom came home and asked me if Stacey and I would be willing to meet with them. I called him at his dorm and told him to plan on it for the following weekend.

Wouldn't you know, that dumbass went to a party that week, got drunk, got in a fight, and got a black eye. When he came home for the weekend and I saw his face, I was mortified. What would this potential adoptive couple think of us? A trailer park trash hoe and her black-eyed boyfriend. I'm sure they would think they HAD to save this baby from whatever fate it may have had with us.

It was almost Christmas when we met them. We visited their home which was perfectly decorated with a beautiful tree. He was a Navy doctor, Irish background. She was a nurse with Italian roots. Their look was similar to ours, as I am half Filipino and Stacey was of the Caucasian variety. I figured if nothing else, our baby would look like it "belonged" to them. They were kind to us, despite Stacey's *Fight Club* look, and they seemed excited and hopeful. As we drove away from their house, I told Stacey and my mom that they were meant to be the baby's parents.

Over the course of my pregnancy, they would call me and ask what I was craving. Then they'd take me and Stacey out to dinner. I thought they were incredibly sophisticated. We went to Olive Garden one night and they had me try calamari for the first time. They took us to our favorite (and expensive) Hibachi-style restaurant, Kyoto, where the chefs chucked shrimp into our mouths as part of their show. I never could catch that damn thing. I grew to love them and I was incredibly excited that they were going to be raising my child.

In the meantime, I was trying to keep my ever-growing belly unnoticed at school. In January, our marching band took its yearly trip to Disney World to march in a parade and frolic carefree in the park. As my friends excitedly headed to Space Mountain, I looked at the precautions on the sign at the entrance to the line. It read:

"WARNING! For safety, you should be in good health and free from high blood pressure, heart, back or neck problems, motion sickness, or other conditions that could be aggravated by this adventure. *Expectant mothers should not ride.*"

I backed away, mumbling some excuse for not wanting to ride. I did that the entire trip.

Things continued to get worse. No matter how hard I tried, the baby was a-growing and I was a-showing. First, I used safety pins on my pants. Then I discovered I could loop a rubber band through the buttonhole and that would add a good three inches of stretch. Then I invested in a LOT of elastic waist shorts. Eventually my protrusion could no longer be denied. People knew I was pregnant.

One day in May, I ducked into a bathroom stall for one of my many potty breaks. It wasn't even one of the bathrooms I typically frequented, but for some reason on that day I ended up in that stall that had the following words scribbled in thick, black Sharpie:

"Stacey Ribino in an knocked up hoe."

My jaw dropped. Tears stung my eyes. I felt like I had been punched in the gut. How insulting! They didn't even spell my name right, or compose a grammatically correct sentence, yet I sat there stunned. This is what people thought of me? This is what people were saying? I angrily left the bathroom and made my way to the guidance counselor's office.

"How many credits do I need to graduate?" I demanded, my B-cup turned C-cup chest heaving.

She thumbed through papers and found whatever she needed. I doubt she knew much about me, but I knew she knew my older sister, the Super Star Valedictorian.

"It looks like you need two credits. An English and a History."

"Then I need information to register for summer school," I told her.

"Now are you sure you want to do that?" she drawled. "Senior year is the time for you to apply to colleges and for financial aid. Your senior year is supposed to be fun. I mean, just look at everything your sister's done. Do you really want to miss out on that?"

"I want to do whatever it takes to get the hell out of this place."

An angry fire ignited in my heart (and no, it wasn't heartburn. At least I don't think it was. Maybe it was.) and raged even more out of control a couple days later when my English teacher took me aside at the end of class. In her hand she held my final paper, ungraded with a yellow sticky note scribbled with some reminder to herself.

"Stacy," she drawled, as she unpeeled the sticky note and set the paper on the desk in front of me, "I can't grade this yet because it seems a lot like something your sister wrote last year. I'm gonna need you to bring hers to me so I can compare the two."

Her thin lipstick-red lips curled into a smug smile that I wanted to smack off her face. I left her classroom practically vibrating with fury. When I met up with Christy at our car at the end of the day, she knew instantly something was wrong. When I told her that I was accused of plagiarizing her paper, she was equally if not more pissed off than me. How dare our teacher think I could write as well as her?! We sped home and she rifled through her files filled with gold stars and A-plus papers. I was never so glad to have a nerd sister who held onto every assignment she had ever done.

The next day I brought the irrefutable proof to my English teacher, haughtily tossing it on her desk. I may have been a trailer park trash, knocked-up hoe, but I was not a plagiarizer. Later, after she graded my paper with the A that it deserved, she offered a tepid apology for her mistake. The damage was done, though, and if I had had any hesitation about graduating a year early, it vanished the moment she slid my final paper across the desk that day. I was ready to say later to the Goose Creek Gators.

A few days later I attended my end-of-the-year band banquet. As a junior, I would have automatically been the drum major again during my senior year. Instead, I "crowned" one of my good friends as the person who would be my replacement. The tradition was that the outgoing senior drum major would walk around the room with one of the ridiculously large, plumed caps we wore as part of our uniform, and place it on the (always shocked but not really shocked) new drum major's head. It had been the same process the year prior when I was crowned as drum major.

After I did that and everyone applauded, I stood at the mic and announced to my fellow band nerds that I was sorry for letting them all down, that I was giving my baby up for adoption, and I would be graduating later in the summer and would not be back for senior year. I looked around the room and saw tears. My band director gave me a huge hug and told me she was proud of me. A couple days later I even got a letter from another teacher, one I had never had, who told me her son was adopted and she was so grateful for people like me. I felt a little less ashamed.

And then Stacey, up to his usual shenanigans, gave me a huge hickey the day before the prom. Yes, at eight months pregnant I still went to my prom. I really didn't want to but my mom talked me into it, persuading me that I needed to do it since I would never have another one. I had had a dress made specially for the occasion (by the same woman who made my drum major uniform, as fate would have it). A trailer park trash hoe in a maternity prom dress with a huge hickey. If you hear banjos strumming when you read that, well I can't say that I blame you.

And then it was the end of the year; the worst, most hellish high school year ever. At graduation I listened to my sister's Valedictorian speech and wondered: how did things end up going so sideways for me? She was so full of hope and positivity; she had a full paid scholarship to college. And I had no clue what was in store for me. All I knew was I had to get this baby out and to its parents.

I started summer school classes right after graduation. The attendance policy was very strict: no more than two absences, period. No exceptions. I knew this was going to be a challenge for me, what with having a baby and all. My due date was the beginning of July so I crossed my fingers the baby would come around the 4th and the holiday would give me some extra time.

No such luck. On the night of June 22nd, I started having what I thought was a horrible stomachache. It kept me up most of the night, and on the toilet a lot. When it finally dawned on me that I might be in labor, I called my mom who was finishing up her swing shift. She had me time the pain which was about every ten minutes. She hurried home and we headed to the hospital.

The adoptive couple was there before we even got there. The adoptive mama fed me ice chips, rubbed my back, and put cool towels on my forehead. I was too far along for an epidural but I was given something else for the pain. Stacey got to the hospital and stayed by my side, watching the rise and fall of my contractions on the monitor. A few more hours of contractions and then I was wheeled into the delivery room. I pushed for what felt like an eternity. And it must have been a long time because when my baby boy finally came, he had the funniest cone-shaped head. I successfully, safely brought him into this world on June 23rd, 1994.

Everything else after that was kind of a blur. I was exhausted. The adoptive couple asked if there was anything I wanted to eat. ANYTHING, they said. Ben and Jerry's Chocolate Fudge Brownie was the first thing that popped into my head. They ran out and bought it, I inhaled it, and then I threw it all back up, all over myself in my hospital bed. It felt like warm chocolate milk had been poured on me.

I was in and out of sleep the rest of the day. A couple people came to visit, some sent flowers, but mostly it was quiet. I guess people don't know how to celebrate adoption. The next morning the attorney came with the papers for us to sign. I held my baby in the crook of my left arm and kissed and cried all over him as I signed away my parental rights to him with my free hand. I spent a miserable night in the hospital, getting woken up by two young male Navy nurses who attempted to give me a catheter but instead ended up giving me a urinary tract infection that would flare up after I was discharged. The next day I got in the car with my mom, and waved goodbye to my beautiful son as his parents held him.

I don't know why I thought it wouldn't hurt as much as it did. I had known all along I was placing him for adoption. I had months to bake him in my belly, and I thought I had done a good job keeping myself detached emotionally. But the instant love I had for him was unexplainable and immeasurable. I had also grown to love the adoptive couple. Driving away from them on the curb of the hospital sidewalk, tears blurring my vision as they grew tinier in the distance, felt like I was leaving a huge part of my heart there with them.

I had him on a Thursday. I was back in summer school the next Monday. A couple months later, I graduated high school.

I wish I could say I went on to do really great things. I did not. Not right away. I fell many times. I always picked myself up and dusted myself off. But it took me a long time to get my life together. When I finally did, I was so excited because it was also when my son would be turning eighteen. I was ready for him to find me and his other siblings. I was proud of my accomplishments and wanted to show him what I had done.

But his 18th birthday came and went, and nothing. Then his 19th. Then his 20th. The phone call never came. No letter, no email, nothing. The years ticked by in silence.

My daughter found him on Facebook and sent him a friend request. He never added her, presumably because he didn't know who she was. I found him on Instagram and started following him. He followed me back and I was thrilled. I thought he would realize who I was and want to connect. In my head, I was planning our first meeting. What I would wear, what I would say. Months went by and… nothing. I messaged him one day and apparently blindsided him. He told me he needed time. That was October 1, 2015. I've messaged him twice more since then, but he hasn't replied. It hurts me that he isn't ready to connect. But that is his decision, and his own story to write. I hope that soon he will want to be a part of my and my family's life. I hope I will be able to re-write this story.

***

Here's the part of the story where I need to insert a record scratch sound effect.

I had started sharing my adoption story in some variation over the last few years, first on an Instagram post, then on Facebook, and I even wrote a blog. In November of 2017 it was published on a website as part of a "Thirty Adoption Stories in Thirty Days" series. In one of my first speaking engagements, I planned to tell my adoption story for the first time in front of an audience. When I told a friend that I was going to share my adoption story as part of my presentation, he cautioned me that I probably shouldn't if I wanted to do business with any of the audience members. I took it to heart, mulled it over, and figured if someone didn't want to do business with me because I was a birth mother then I probably didn't want to do business with them. It was a risk I was willing to take.

The day of my presentation, I gulped down a glass of water and wiped my sweaty palms on my skirt as I went to the front of the room. For nearly forty-five minutes, I made myself completely vulnerable in front of the crowd of about sixty real estate professionals. I literally ended my presentation with the words, "Welp, that's all I got." Everyone applauded and I sat back down. When the meeting concluded, a line of people approached me to shake my hand, hug me, and share their own stories of mistakes turned right. I was shocked. I had been so worried that people would judge me; instead they embraced me. I started getting invitations for more speaking gigs, and I realized I LOVED speaking. That was the beginning of the journey toward my speaking career, all because I was brave enough to share my adoption story.

I crafted an analogy about cultivating pearls from our past that I started using in my speeches. A pearl, after all, is the end result of a negative situation. An irritant, like a grain of sand, gets into a mollusk's shell. The soft, fleshy mollusk, in an effort to protect itself from said irritant, creates a sac and then covers it with layer upon layer of an iridescent substance called mother-of-pearl. This process ends with a shiny, beautiful pearl. I likened my story of being called a "knocked-up hoe" and how that rattled around in my head and my heart for years, until one day I re-examined it and found the pearl that I called "badass birth mother." I challenged audience members to think of the bad, hurtful parts of their pasts and see if they could re-evaluate them to see them as positive and beautiful.

I shared this message over and over, in every presentation, on my social media, to anyone who would listen. Create your pearls, I would say. Own your story. Be brave. It became one of my signature talking points and a core value in my coaching business. But I had to get really honest with myself about how true to this message I was really living.

I had been telling myself (and been told by others) for almost two years that I should write a book. I even started to do it on several occasions. But I always got hung up before I got too deep into it because I knew there were still secrets I had yet to share, and I was terrified of what people would think of me if and when I shared those. Starting with my adoption story.

Every part of the story was true yet, by simple omission, there was one ginormous piece of information that changed everything. Yes, Stacey was my high school sweetheart. We were together when I found out I was pregnant; we were together when we chose the adoptive couple; we were together when we signed the papers relinquishing any and all rights to the baby. The picture I have from the hospital bed on the day we said our goodbyes to our baby is of me and Stacey. We, as two teenage kids, experienced the pregnancy, the judgment, the pain, the ups and downs of the entire process. But the thing that gnawed at me the whole time, and the thing that I knew to be absolute truth when I found my son on Instagram in 2015 and took one look at his handsome face, was that he looked remarkably like his dad. And his dad was not Stacey.

I know, I know. What a slutbucket. If I could have that part of the story voiced over by Morgan Freeman or the sexy Latino voice from "Jane the Virgin," I think that would help lighten up the heaviness just a bit. If you can read it in either one of those voices, that would be great. Seriously, though—that was a very heavy load to carry for so long. No matter what positive changes I made in life or how "good" a person I became, I was always haunted by the mistakes made by my sixteen-year-old self. And I had been telling the story for years, feeling sleazy as the lie slid out of my mouth every time I said my high school sweetheart Stacey was the baby's dad.

Remember how I was the drum major of the marching band? There was a cute boy from a local college who had been hired to come work with the percussionists. I thought he was the bee's knees. I was one of a few girls he flirted with, and as the marching season went along, so did the seriousness of the flirtations. (This all happened during one of the many breakups I had had with Stacey, so I was single and ready to mingle.) While he wasn't a teacher at our school, I'm sure there were still some rules about him canoodling with any of the students. For that reason, not to mention the legalities around our age difference, we kept it under very tight wraps when we started dating.

It was an exciting relationship, him sneaking over to the trailer and me sneaking over to his dorm room. I adored what I considered to be his college sophistication and I loved that he was a fellow musician although, as a percussionist, he had a very annoying habit of tapping out rhythmic cadences on my arms or legs as he imaginarily riffed and rat-a-tatted drum solos. He also still flirted with a few other girls in the band which drove me crazy, but he assured me it was only to keep up appearances so the band director wouldn't suspect that there was something going on between us. One time we got all fancied up and went to the symphony. It sucked that I couldn't tell any of my friends about it afterward.

At a marching band competition one night, after we had performed our show and we were seated back in the bleachers awaiting the announcement of the results, Stacey appeared in the crowd of spectators. He had driven the two hours from his college to surprise me. All my friends, who knew nothing of the relationship I had with the percussion assistant, oohed and ahhed the wildly romantic gesture. Admittedly, I was pretty swept away too.

My history with Stacey was like a boomerang that, no matter how many times we threw it away, always came back to us. After the awards ceremony, giddy from our victory, I wasn't even a little surprised when Stacey showed up on the front porch of my trailer. I told him I had been dating someone, he told me he didn't care, we had sex on the floor of my living room while the rest of my family was asleep (sorry, mom!), and the next day I broke up with the drummer boy. When I found out I was pregnant a month later, a tiny flicker of panic ignited in my chest. There is no feeling quite like that when you pee on a stick, the plus sign appears, and you think, "Shiiiiiiiiiit."

Since we were giving the baby up for adoption, a part of my brain rationalized that the paternity of the baby didn't matter. I realize how irresponsibly shitty that may sound now. At the time, the percussion assistant could have gotten in major trouble for statutory rape. When I told him I was pregnant and he asked if it was his, I was truthful and told him I wasn't one hundred percent positive, that it was either his or Stacey's. Since I was already back together with Stacey and since he didn't want to ruin his entire future over a short-lived high school fling, we decided to part ways amicably as if nothing had ever happened. I'm sure he wanted the baby to be Stacey's as much or more than I did. Many years later in our relationship, Stacey asked me if the baby had even been his. I admitted that I didn't think he was. This was one of the heaviest and hardest truths I carried throughout my life and it was amplified when Stacey passed away in 2017. I didn't admit the details of this heinous offense to my own family until 2018.

My birth son has made no attempt to contact me and I don't know if he ever will. But if and when that day comes, I will have a hell of a story for him: one in which his dad, the man who signed the adoption papers and endured the heartbreak of handing him to his adoptive parents, died after a battle with cancer; and one in which his biological dad is very much alive and, from what I gathered from my Facebook stalking, is happily married to a lovely woman, with four beautiful kids, and working in his calling as a musician.

The burden of the shame I have carried along with this secret was somewhat lessened when I unloaded it onto my husband and my grown daughter, both of whom actually seemed way more nonchalant about it than I had anticipated. I guess they weren't shocked to hear about what a slutty sixteen-year-old I was. Besides, I think when there's enough time and distance from anything, the once pointy edges of the truth become blurred and dull, and with it the hurt caused by it. I worry that one day my son will decide to find out about me and his dad. And when he does, that truth will set in motion a series of changes for a whole other family. But then again, I might be worrying about something that may not ever happen after all.

CHAPTER EIGHT:
BAD MOM

"Don't judge me so harsh little girl
You got a playboy mommy, come home
But when you tell them soldiers my name
Cross that bridge all on your own
Little girl they'll do you no harm
They know your playboy mommy
But I'll be home
I'll be home to take you in my arms"
~Tori Amos, "Playboy Mommy"

It's Mother's Day 2019 and, while I've recently been on a bit of an alcohol abstinence, today I've had a few "Mom-osas"—basically a mimosa cocktail on steroids that's ninety percent champagne, ten percent orange juice. I once saw a viral video about a bar that featured this exact libation, but they called it a "Man-mosa." It was an entire 750 ml bottle of champagne (which, let's be honest, is mostly just bubbles) and a splash of OJ. I think they missed out on a huge opportunity to market to their mama demographic. No one needs/deserves this bubbly magic more than those brave, badass souls. And for the non-alcohol-drinking segment of moms out there: Kudos to you for having the fortitude to get through this time without the occasional glass of stress-relieving wine or endorphin-producing mojito.

I know how this must sound: Wow, Stacy can't deal so she totally relies on alcohol as a crutch. You're not wrong. In fact, this is exactly why, in 2018, I took multiple thirty-day alcohol sabbaticals and am now toying with the idea of giving up alcohol altogether. I'll be the first to admit that for me, when the going gets tough the tough turn to alcohol. I am the "tough" in that equation. And you know what's really tough? Parenting. Especially *special needs* parenting. When people ask me "How do you do it?" I'm only half-joking when I answer, "Running and copious amounts of wine."

In 2017, I read *The Compound Effect* by Darren Hardy and he addressed this phenomenon, recommending a thirty-day break from anything you may consider to be a vice. Basically, the premise is: if you think something in your life is problematic, take a thirty-day break from said weakness to prove you have control over it. In the spring and then again in the fall of 2018, I did this, first with alcohol and then with alcohol *and* Facebook. Why? Because I felt like I might be addicted to both and was worried about the ramifications of each. I associated alcohol with both positive and negative life events, using it as a crutch during hard times but also as something celebratory during good times.

With Haiden specifically, I could tell as my stress barometer rose, so did the likelihood of me cracking open and consuming an entire bottle of Malbec on any given day of the week. When I received a call from the principal's office, when he had a meltdown during his ABA session, when he lashed out at me over anything—I immediately wanted to seek solace in the non-judgmental comfort of a bottle of wine. Alcohol was a coping mechanism, offering a short-lived reprieve from the sometimes unbearable overwhelm I felt on a daily basis. I wouldn't say I drank too much but I definitely felt like the frequency was becoming problematic. And the older I got, the more I felt it the following morning, often dragging ass the majority of the next day. Ain't nobody got time for that!

I had my first drink at a party with Stacey when he was a senior and I was a freshman. Someone mixed a very strong Crown Royal with RC Cola in a plastic Big Gulp cup from 7-11. I drank it on an empty stomach, nervous in the presence of some of my high school's most popular kids. Later, as I vomited what felt like everything I had ever consumed in my life, I swore to the Good Lord above I'd never drink again if I survived that miserable night. If I had a dollar for every time I had made this proclamation as I prayed to the porcelain god, I would have had a lot of dollars.

I didn't drink a ton in high school, but after I had my baby and gave him up for adoption, I definitely started to spiral. I had some major depression on top of the trauma I had experienced from my sexual abuse, and alcohol helped numb the pain. A few weeks after the adoption, Stacey and I went to Myrtle Beach with a few of his friends. They were all drinking beer, which at the time I hated, so Stacey grabbed a six-pack of Zima for me. Zima was a malted beverage that tasted like watered down Sprite and low self-esteem. I drank myself into an oblivion that ended with me laughing like a madwoman until I broke down sobbing. Then I passed out. I started seeking this euphoria as often as possible. By the fall of 1994, a few months before my eighteenth birthday, it had gotten so bad that my mom kicked me out of the house. That was one of the first times I slipped closer to what would eventually be my Rock Bottom.

When my sister came home from her first semester at Brigham Young University and saw what a shambles my life was, she begged me to move to Utah with her. In Provo, Utah, often called "Happy Valley" for its high concentration of bright-eyed, righteous Mormons (ahem, Latter-Day Saints), surely a lost soul like mine could be found. Plus, I think she wanted to have a car there and since she couldn't afford her own, having mine there was the next best thing. I was just part of the package deal. There was an opening for a roommate in her apartment, so I figured what the hell and I packed up my Nissan Sentra with what little belongings I had and we headed west. When we got there, we found out someone else had signed the contract for the apartment, so now I was thousands of miles from home and homeless.

I ended up finding an apartment with five other girls in a BYU-approved complex. I was obviously NOT a BYU student, so I had to show intent that I would register for the other local college, Utah Valley State College. Trying to fit in and please my sister, I started going to church with my roommates. I hated it. I hadn't gone since my parents' divorce a few years prior and when I felt forced into it again, resentment bubbled up in me. I felt betrayed by the religion and befuddled by the repentance process in which I was forced to sit before of group of strange men and answer their interrogation into my past transgressions. I was told to pray and read the scriptures and that I would be filled with the bright light of Christ. Much as I tried, the light never ignited within me. When I told one of my roommates about it, her reply was, "Fake it 'til you make it." Clearly, I was not a good enough actor to play the part.

I started taking classes at UVSC and got a job at the local Sears store working in the Domestics Department. It was boring AF but my roommate Amber worked there and she was a delight. She desperately wanted to help me find my way back to the straight and narrow path of righteousness, so she set me up with one of our co-workers. He was recently back from an LDS mission to Japan and was now on a mission to find a wife. We started an unlikely courtship and, as I shared stories from my past, he made it clear that I was lucky to have found him on my journey to salvation. After a few short months of dating, we got engaged. Shortly after that, I found out I was pregnant which, according to him, was mostly my fault considering all my recent sins.

He used my past as a means to manipulate me, to remind me of my unworthiness, and to place blame for his own transgressions. He food-shamed me often, criticizing what and how much I ate which, at the time, wasn't very much. One day when I battled morning sickness, having only consumed a few saltines and some Sprite, he came home from work and asked me if I was going to the gym. I could barely get my ass out of bed. I dropped out of school and secretly plotted my escape. He accounted for all the money I made at Sears, so I sold my textbooks and squirreled away what little money I could. Ring on my finger, his baby in my belly, I felt trapped like a wild animal in a cage. As much as I wanted out, I couldn't see any feasible options.

Our wedding was planned for June in South Carolina, an embarrassment for him since it wouldn't be performed in the sanctity of an LDS temple. A few of my mom's family members made the trip from New Jersey; none of his family came. That ended up being a smart decision on their part as it would have been a waste of money. I accidentally (subconsciously?) forgot to pick up our marriage license the day before the ceremony. After he screamed at me, calling me all sorts of names as I cried, I asked him why he even wanted to marry me. He couldn't come up with any sort of answer that included the word 'love,' so he stormed off to his hotel and started packing his bags. My mom, who saw the way he treated me and never cared for him in the first place, returned the favor I had given her when she got pregnant with my baby sister a few years prior.

"You don't have to stay with him just because you're pregnant," she told me. There it was, there was my out.

I cried even harder then, but my tears were tears of sweet relief.

On the day we were supposed to get married, he boarded the plane back to Utah and my family threw me a party at our house on Bayberry Drive. My aunt Kathy, who had made our wedding cake, iced what would have been the middle of the three-tiered masterpiece. In her tasty homemade blue frosting she wrote "Congratulations" with an X through it; right below that she wrote "Never Mind." Man, I loved my aunt Kathy. She died of ALS a few years later, the first of three of my mom's relatives to lose the same battle.

That was the summer I got back together with Stacey, and y'all already know how that story went down. Meanwhile, Mia's dad had indeed attained the temple wedding he had wanted. I only found out when I attempted to get child support from him when Mia was almost two and he denied paternity. She and I had to go to a designated lab and have swabs taken from the lining of our mouths. The technician, who happened to be from my old church, told me that was likely what had happened; that he was probably married and trying to cover his ass. By the time the results came back confirming that he was her dad, she and I had moved from South Carolina back to Utah.

One day I took Mia shoe shopping and we stopped into the Sears where I used to work. For some reason, it never dawned on me that her dad might still work there. Mia was intent on finding some Dora the Explorer shoes, so she was super annoyed when I was stopped by a tall stranger who couldn't stop staring at her. That was the first day he ever laid eyes on her, probably hoping to find a child who looked nothing like him. I imagine he was shitting some major bricks when he saw the striking similarities, wondering how he was going to explain this to his wife. A couple weeks later, after the paternity results were in, he called me at my job at Outback Steakhouse to "let me know she was his." I rolled my eyes and nearly broke the phone off the wall when I hung up. And I know what you're thinking after the truth bomb in the last chapter. But I was on the path to redemption when I got knocked up by the returned missionary! There was definitely no other contender in the sperm donor department.

From then on, he and his wife wanted to be in her life. They started taking her on weekends, then every other week, then two weeks at a time. By the time she started school, they wanted to have her full time. We had a heated debate about it, which included him growling, "I'm going to make sure she grows up to be nothing like you." When all was said and done, I acquiesced and let him register her for kindergarten. His wife was a stay-at-home mom and I was working full-time and going to school. I was also failing in the relationship department and a tiny part of me thought maybe she *would* be better off being nothing like me. When he later got a job offer in Washington, I made the hard decision that I thought was the best for her at the time and let him take her with them. I always regretted that decision but also believed strongly in the saying: "If you love something set it free. If it comes back it's yours. If not, it was never meant to be." I always hoped she would come back to me.

In 2015, she finally did.

***

I never thought I would be a Soccer Mom. Since Mia had grown up with her dad and stepmom in another state, I never had the pleasure (responsibility) of watching her do any sort of extracurriculars. Haiden is autistic, was not very coordinated, and was about as interested in sports as a fish is interested in breathing out-of-water. But the caboose to our crazy train, our little Eli Guy, was the genetic replica of his daddy and was therefore signed up for soccer, baseball and basketball at six years old. I was a band nerd growing up, so the extent of my athletic abilities was knowing when to play the school fight song at football games. Even then, I usually needed my co-drum major Willie to prompt me when we had scored a touchdown. So while I had never dreamt in my wildest fantasies I'd be living the glam life of a sports mom, I sure as hell didn't think I'd be a grandma in the same year.

When Mia came to live with us in 2015, she was going through some tumultuous times in her life. She was miserable in school at BYU-Idaho and was in love with a non-Mormon Marine who was finishing up his basic training. A week into her second semester of school, she called me and begged me to come get her. This was the moment I had been waiting for since the day she left with her dad more than ten years prior. I sped up to Idaho, loaded her belongings into my car, and brought her back home. Her dad and stepmom were not happy with her decision, cutting off any and all financial help as well as familial ties. She struggled with being cut off and threw herself into her long-distance relationship with Bailey.

He came for a visit in March and they talked about getting engaged. Shortly after that, they announced they were getting married in May. With only about six weeks to plan, we scrambled to put together a small, lovely ceremony. Bailey flew into town and surprised her at work on a Thursday, placing a beautiful ring on her finger at David's Bridal. On Sunday, they exchanged vows in a charming restaurant in front of friends and family. Her dad and stepmom and a few of her dad's side of the family came. Most of them were cordial to me and my family, but her dad and stepmom wouldn't even look at me. I drank a bunch of champagne and pretended it wasn't awkward AF that we were in such close proximity but acted like we weren't in the same room. All those years ago, I wished we could have been cool co-parents; it wasn't in the cards and now that she was a married woman, there was no need to even try.

Mia lived with us for a little longer until Bailey finished tech school and they got stationed in Colorado. They were there for a couple years when he got orders to deploy. Rather than spend her time alone on base, I invited her to come stay with us while he was gone. They enjoyed the Christmas and New Year's holidays together before he packed up and shipped off.

A few weeks later, on January 28th, 2018, I celebrated my 41st birthday. Three days later, Mia came into my bedroom with a stricken expression on her face. She plopped down beside me on my bed, handed me her phone, and asked, "Does that look positive to you?" I looked at the picture of the pregnancy test and saw two faint lines. "Oh. Fuck," I said. Mia burst into tears. Apparently, she and her husband had *really* enjoyed their holidays. While she openly freaked out, I inwardly freaked out. The panicked feeling was not unlike the one I had felt the first time I had peed on a stick and those two ominous lines magically appeared two minutes later.

In all fairness, Mia and Bailey had been married for almost three years and it was bound to happen sooner or later. (I would have been okay with it being a *little* bit later.) But I did ask her to wait until I was at least forty (she did) which was more than I had done for my own mom. Besides, everyone told me being a grandma was "The Best" and I would be a cool, hot grandma. How many other grandmas ran marathons?? (Disclosure: I actually know quite a few.)

I spent the majority of the year mentally preparing for my

upcoming role of grandmotherhood. We decided "grandma" was too matronly for me and found out the Filipino term for grandma was "Lola." I decided to embrace my very watered-down Filipino heritage and opted for this title. As far as hip grandma names go, this one seemed like the best one for me.

We had planned a family trip to Maui for my husband's birthday in October but, realizing how close Mia's due date was ("Happy 40th Birthday, Dusty! You're gonna be a grandpa!"), we rescheduled it for mid-September. Mia decided she would be too pregnant and their finances too tight for her to join us in Maui. I worried about leaving her alone and made her promise not to go into labor while we were gone.

We spent five days in the most humid, most magical place we'd ever been, surrounded by more Filipinas than I had seen since my days growing up as a Navy brat on the east coast. I had nearly forgotten how unfiltered some Asian women were until one day I was souvenir-shopping in Lahaina. I had discovered a little store that sold mini bottles and rejoiced when I realized I didn't have to spend $14 on every drink at the hotel when I could make my own for much cheaper. I placed a few of the prized mini bottles and a four-pack of pineapple juice on the counter, along with a treat that Eli had asked for. He stood next to me, impatiently waiting for the container of mini M&Ms.

The cashier, a tiny Asian lady who could have fit in my pocket, peered over her glasses at Eli and then looked up at me. She asked for my I.D. which made me happy—she obviously must have thought I was young. I got that a lot. She handed back my license and said in a thick accent, "Is he your son?" I figured she was curious since I had brown eyes and golden-brown skin and he was a blonde-haired, blue-eyed kid. When I told her yes, she dryly replied, "You are too old to be his mother." Ouch! Those crazy Asians pack a punch. I took my bruised ego out of the store to find my husband, whose fault it was that I was an old mom.

When I met Dusty in 2009, I had gone through my third divorce, had two kids by two different dads (one of whom I hadn't even married), and had absolutely zero intention of ever remarrying and definitely wasn't going to have more kids. Dusty, who had been a perpetual bachelor for thirty-one years, posed little threat to me since I figured I'd just be one of the many women he casually dated. As things started getting more serious, I got a little panicky when, one night on the way to a friend's house, he casually told me he wanted to have "at least" three kids. If he was thinking of a future with me, that math would not add up.

After dating for over a year, we came to a completely non-climactic agreement: I told him I'd be willing to have one more baby and he told me he'd be happy if we didn't have anymore. It was like a weird version of the Gift of the Magi. After we got engaged in July of 2011, I decided to go off birth control. I was thirty-four and in college, my fourth attempt at getting a bachelor's degree, but figured I wasn't getting any younger, so what the hell. Plus, it had taken over a year to get pregnant with Haiden and my biological clock was ticking hard. Dusty must have had some good swimmers, because by October my eggo was prego with Eli.

And that is how I came to be a 42-year-old mom to a 23-year-old daughter, a 14-year-old son, and a 7-year-old son; and grandmother to an 11-month-old grandson. My older sister Christy is a year and eleven days older than me. Then there's a seven-year gap between me and my next brother, Alex. The age gap between me and my youngest brother Josh is eleven years, and my younger sister Jody is fifteen years. There are pros and cons to having kids close together and having them far apart. As it sits from my perspective, I'm going to be a mom FOREVER. There's also a high likelihood that my Haiden might live with us indefinitely. I've come to accept all these facts. The major identity crisis lies in who the hell I am from moment to moment, day to day, as a wife, mom, grandma, and budding entrepreneur who has only recently discovered her life's purpose. That's where I currently reside, on the corner of "I've Only Just Begun" and "Holy Shit, I'm a Grandma."

There is a part of me that takes great pleasure in watching someone's jaw drop when I tell them I'm a grandma. They're usually shocked, or at least are really good at pretending to be shocked. In either case, it's a huge ego boost so I willingly accept it. And the same can be said when I tell people I have a 23-year-old daughter. "Nooooo," they typically say. "Did you have her when you were five? How do you stay so young-looking?" Again, my secret is a combination of wine, Oil of Olay, and running.

I feel like each of my kids has gotten such a different version of me and there's a lot of guilt I have around that. The son I gave up for adoption, then relinquishing custody of Mia— I feel like I lost those two altogether. The mom Haiden got started out rocky but pulled it together after a few years. And now Eli gets the version of World's Okayest Mom, who's trying her best to be rad but who also wants to spread her wings and soar. The Momming gig is hard; it's a tricky balancing act. Hell, just getting this many words together in one space has taken time away from them. But this mama bear has badassery to attend to. My kids are turning out to be rad humans, so I can't be screwing things up too much, right?

And I am SO glad social media wasn't around when I traipsed and tripped through the early days of motherhood because mom-shaming is brutal. I would have gotten eaten alive. No, I'm too smart for that. Instead, I'm writing a book chronicling not only my mom fails, but many other failures too. Feast on this, shamers!

Seriously, though. I think I've made a little bit of a redemption. Yes, I used to leave Mia with a babysitter and try to sneak my underage ass into bars. Now, I'm sneaking into boardrooms and bringing my minority woman voice to the table. And yes, I used to be on government assistance. Today, I'm the founder of a nonprofit. I wouldn't have gotten to where I am today had I not gone through the muck I did to get here. Each of those experiences served a purpose. I dug a hole, I fell in, and I climbed my way back out. My kids inspired me to find my Why, they filled me with a sense of purpose. And my legacy is for them.

So, cheers. Cheers to the years on welfare; cheers to heartbreaks and losses; cheers to finally finding the right hubby; cheers to my kids who make me a better person every day; cheers to the miles it took to get here; cheers to discovering my purpose; cheers to the courage to share the things we don't talk about.

CHAPTER NINE:
DEHUMANIZATION

"Eliminate the concept of division by class, skills, race, income, and nationality. We are all equals with a common pulse to survive. Every human requires food and water. Every human has a dream and desire to be happy. Every human responds to love, suffering and pain. Every human bleeds the same color and occupies the same world. Let us recognize that we are all part of each other. We are all human. We are all one."
~Suzy Kassem, writer, director, philosopher, poet, and citizen of the world

Even though Christy and I are one year and eleven days apart, my mom used to dress us in matching outfits like we were twins. Occasionally she'd get the same outfit in different colors—like the cute striped dresses we wore to Sea World, one dark pink the other teal—but for the most part they were identical. Considering that we shared clothes, it would have made more sense financially to buy different outfits rather than two of the same things. But it was the 80s and I think we can all agree that questionable choices were made by everyone back then.

When I was three, we fostered a set of twin girls, Shelly and Kelly. Now my mom had the real chance to dress twins in matching clothes, but did that mean Christy and I were off the hook? Nope. Mom still dressed us like the creepy girls from "The Shining" and now, when we went out in public, strangers would ooh and ahh and ask, "You have *two* sets of twins?" We were like a traveling circus act everywhere we went.

We had Shelly and Kelly pretty much from their birth until they were almost eighteen months old. My parents wanted to adopt them and had tried starting the process but were denied. The agency wanted the girls to end up with a family more racially suited for them—and that meant a family with at least one black parent. The girls' birth mom was Black and, while there was no confirmation on bio dad, we believed they were bi-racial. I didn't understand any of this as a young girl. I knew that they had kinky curly hair that I loved and their skin color was a mocha shade just a titch darker than my own. I cried watching my mom cry the day some grownups showed up at our house and whisked Shelly and Kelly away.

It's a strange feeling when you realize someone can judge, stereotype, fear or hate you based solely on the color of your skin. The first memory I have of hearing the word "racist" was when we got stationed in Langley, Virginia when I was in the second grade. We had arrived at our new apartment complex ahead of our dad, so my mom did the first thing she always did when we got to a new place: she looked up the number to the local LDS church and found out what time they convened. Not knowing a soul, we showed up to church on Sunday, my White mother with her two brown daughters and one brown son. Congregation members welcomed us into their fold that day and the next Sunday. But when my dad finally joined us and came to church with us that third Sunday, many of the members turned cold.

I didn't notice it at the time, but later I overheard my mom talking to my dad about it. She was confused by the change in temperament and concluded that maybe they were racist. Maybe they didn't like that she, a Caucasian woman, was married to a Filipino man. It was of no concern to me then; I was more interested in things like getting the newest pink and gray Huffy bicycle, or the suit you could put on Cabbage Patch Kids dolls that made them poseable. Racism was far from my radar.

Until middle school, my skin color and features were of no consequence to me. We moved around a lot with the military, and we fit in easily in the schools in New Jersey, California, Virginia, and South Carolina. My appearance wasn't important to me as a carefree child who wanted nothing more than to explore whatever new surroundings we found ourselves in. But man, once those pre-teen years hit, I became obsessed with my looks.

My music idols were Debbie Gibson and Tiffany. My favorite show was Beverly Hills 90210. My best friends had blonde hair and blue eyes, and that's what I wanted to look like more than anything. I wore powdered foundation that was two shades lighter than my natural skin color. I put Sun-In on my hair, desperately trying to lighten my dark brown hair. I didn't even like boys who looked anything like me and couldn't understand my White friends who liked Filipino boys. Blech. I liked boys with blue eyes, white skin and any shade of hair from blonde to ginger.

I hated my flat, Filipino nose and spent hours trying to pinch my nostrils together in an attempt to train my nose to look more like a White girl's. Once, at a sleepover with my BFFs, we giggled as we attempted goofy things like going cross-eyed (I was great at that), rolling our tongues into taco shapes (I still, for the life of me, can't do this), and flaring our nostrils. We took turns going around the room showing off our skills (or lack of them). When it was my turn to flare my nostrils, no matter how hard I tried, I couldn't do it. I shrugged and said, "Oh well. I guess I don't know how to flare my nostrils." "It's okay," one of my friends consoled. "Your nostrils look like they're *always* flared."

I became hyper conscious about my looks in my teenage years, especially since I felt like I was forever in my sister's shadow. A church member once told me casually, "I have the hardest time telling you two apart, so I just remember that you're the fat one." A rebellious, leather-jacketed boy I had dated for a little while (and then dumped) wrote in Christy's yearbook: "To the nicer, prettier of The Rabino Twins..." And on a phone call with a boy from James Island who I had the biggest crush on, he asked what my favorite feature was. When I told him I liked my eyes, he replied, "What's so special about your eyes? They're shit brown."

In high school my feelings shifted a little when I started dating Stacey. Stacey LOVED Filipinas. He was like a groupie and always had a ton of Filipinas around him. When he chose me as HIS Filipina, well butter my biscuit if that wasn't the most flattering feeling. He truly made me feel like the most beautiful person in the world. But even with him, sometimes the racial differences between us surfaced. Like when we went to his family reunion and he warned me that I might get called a "sand nigger" by his relatives.

Goose Creek was fairly racially diverse, but it was the south and we still had our fair share of Confederate flag fanatics. I never thought about skin color as a determining factor in my friendships— Black, White, Asian, they were all my friends. But occasionally, I felt a little like a misfit because I was a "half breed." In Harry Potter terms, I was a Muggle, a Mudblood; only without the perk of magical abilities. I didn't totally fit in with my White friends, nor did I qualify as a real Pinoy. Once my dad was out of the picture, I definitely felt less Filipino. I got asked all the time if I spoke the native language, Tagalog, or if I cooked any of the traditional dishes. I only knew a few swear words my friends had taught me and only knew how to make lumpia, Filipino egg rolls.

When I moved to Utah, I became even more aware of my "brownness." I was often asked where I was from. When I answered "New Jersey" it was almost comical watching people's blank expressions. "Do you mean 'what's my ethnicity'?" I would ask. Sometimes the question from strangers was even tackier: "What *are* you?" People often liked to guess and I got everything from Tongan, Samoan, Mexican, Korean, Native American, Hawaiian, and Black. I joked with a half-Japanese friend at work one night and we came up with "Blackanese" as our new ethnicity.

If my life was a horror movie, as the Token Asian, I'd be one of the first characters to get killed. (But only after I calculated some crazy mathematical equations and drove a car like a madwoman first. Because stereotypes.) This is the thought I have sometimes when I'm the only brown person in the room—and it's not uncommon that I am, indeed, the only POC (person of color) in certain settings. Women in Business groups, board meetings, committee meetings, Body Pump classes. When I submitted my application to serve as a director on a board for my alma mater, I waited anxiously to hear if I had been accepted. My friend who had nominated me said, "No need to worry. You're a woman and a minority. Of course they'll pick you." As if none of my other accomplishments mattered since I checked off those two boxes.

I've been on the minority side of reverse discrimination, so I totally get the concept of "filling a quota." During my second attempt at college in 1996, I planned on following in my mom's footsteps and going into the nursing program at the local technical college. I knew there was a two- to three-year waitlist, so I signed up for it as soon as I started my first semester of general credits. Imagine my surprise when I received notification at the end of my second semester that I had been accepted to the program and could start taking nursing classes right away. The years I had planned on using to mentally prepare for the rigors of nursing school vanished instantly. Naturally I made the decision to first: freak out and second: drop out.

Sometimes being a minority worked for me; other times it worked against me. In any case, I never wanted to "play any cards" to get something I didn't deserve. I also didn't want to be dismissed, overlooked, shot down or shut up due to my race or gender either. It's a slippery slope and I find myself uncomfortable both when I am quiet and when I am vocal about it.

I once went to a sales presentation for a real estate brokerage that was notoriously "Mad Men." A friend who had worked there previously told me the broker required the female employees to wear dresses or skirts. This was in 2017, not 1957. As the group of Realtors gathered in the conference room—eight men and one woman, all White—one of the men started making Indian jokes. Well, the punch lines were about Indians but the dumb jokes were about Native Americans. Something about teepees? And making reservations? All I know is the jokes were super lame, inappropriate, and they left me feeling very unsettled. The fact that everyone in that room laughed and didn't seem to think there was anything wrong with what was being said told me everything I needed to know about my place on their hierarchy.

I spent nearly two decades in the service industry, waiting tables and bartending at just about every establishment under the sun. Sizzler, Outback Steakhouse, Olive Garden, Red Lobster, Applebee's, Boston's, and a ton of local joints as well. I have been on the receiving end of some pretty deplorable behavior that almost led me to losing hope in the future of humanity. I could compile a whole other book about some of the atrocities I've seen, but I'll condense it down to this nice, bulleted list for your reading pleasure:

- "I tithe ten percent to God. Why should I tip my server more than that?" You're giving ten percent of your *entire* income to God. Servers deserve (at least) twenty percent of your dinner bill. It's a significantly smaller amount of money and, honestly, shouldn't even be an argument if you are, in fact, an upstanding churchgoer of any religion.
- Leaving a business card, religious pamphlet, or any other printed paraphernalia made to look like a folded twenty-, fifty- or hundred-dollar-bill if you don't actually leave that big of a tip. Just don't. I'm pretty sure even Jesus thinks this is a

totally uncool and stupid marketing ploy. Really bad way to proselytize.

- Ordering a refill of the Never-Ending-Pasta-Bowl and immediately asking for a to-go box, knowing damn well you can't take a to-go box. It says so on the table tent. And then leaving a penny as the tip, written in on the credit card slip. There's a special place in hell for people who do this.

- When your steak is undercooked but you refuse to send it back to the kitchen to be cooked more because you watched a "20/20" episode about spiteful cooks spitting on food, so you demand an entirely new steak be cooked instead, you actually *increase* the chances of pissing off the cook and thereby ending up with saliva seasoning on your ribeye. Logic, people.

- Screaming at a host, server, busser, bartender or any other restaurant staff about, well, anything. Ever. It's absolutely uncalled for. The way you treat others is a reflection on you, not them. And if you are the type of person who talks down to those around you, especially about something as trivial as fried mozzarella sticks, you are an A-hole of the biggest kind. Never bite the hand that feeds you. Literally.

I'm not saying that these experiences had anything to do with me being brown or a woman or a brown woman. *Although there has been research that shows:

1. "Female servers are being held to a very high standard, and if this standard is not met, they are treated unfavorably in comparison to male servers who produce the same level of service quality." (Matthew Parrett, "Customer Discrimination in Restaurants: Dining Frequency Matters," *Journal of Labor Research* 32, no. 2 (2011): 100-103.)

2. "Larger breast size, blond hair and relative youth correlate with higher tips for waitresses." (Michael Lynn, "Determinants and Consequences of Female Attractiveness and Sexiness: Realistic Tests with Restaurant Waitresses," *Archives of Sexual Behavior* 38 (2009): 737-745.)

3. "There is still a $4 per hour wage gap between what white workers and workers of color make in the restaurant industry, and it's because workers of color are relegated to lower-level positions. In fine dining, they work as bussers and runners,

instead of as servers and bartenders. They also work in lower-level segments, at places like Olive Garden instead of at places like Capital Grille. They work in places where you make less money." (Roberto A. Ferdman, "I dare you to read this and still feel good about tipping," *The Washington Post.* February 18, 2016.)

But worse than racism or sexism: my experiences were *dehumanizing.* I've been treated like an absolute nobody which is almost worse than being treated like garbage. At least when I've been treated like trash, they're acknowledging my (obviously intolerable) existence. Years of experiences like this, paired with my already diminished self-esteem, kept me locked in a spiral of perpetual shame. I was a Nobody. Easily replaceable, a cog in a machine, expendable, disposable, and utterly forgettable.

Test this out the next time you go to eat: Look at your server. Engage with them. When they greet you with "How are you today?" don't reply with "I'll have a Diet Coke with a lemon." Talk to them. They are people. You are, presumably, a person. It shouldn't be so hard. And know that if you are the perpetrator of any of the aforementioned offenses, you're likely assuming the role of "That Asshole at Table 22" in someone else's story.

When I was a Realtor, I was constantly schmoozed by loan officers and title companies who wanted me to send them my business. There was one loan officer who would stop by my office pretty regularly, sticky sweet with her ass-kissing to me and every other Realtor in the building. One day she came with some of her clients to the brewery where I worked (while I waited for the "Big Break" in my real estate career). When I approached her table with a warm, "Hi, how are you?" she barely glanced at me before curtly ordering her drink.

I walked back into the kitchen and checked out the mirror that hung above the employee hand-washing sink. Yup, I definitely looked like myself. I mean, I wore a black T-shirt with a rooster screen-printed on it instead of a business casual outfit, but it wasn't that clever of a disguise that she shouldn't have recognized me. It was such a fascinating phenomenon, watching her from "the other side" of the table in her natural habitat. I never caught that big real estate break, but even if I had, she never would've gotten my business.

I worked at Teppanyaki during the market crash of 2008, as my

Realtor stint fizzled out. I was amazed that people could still afford to eat at this pricey establishment, but even in down times, people loved their flying shrimp. Aside from the hibachi and sushi chefs, and two managers, I was one of the only Asian servers. I joked that my customers were delighted to get a "Real One" when I showed up to the table in my kimono uniform, complete with white socks and black flip flops. One night when I was off work, my friend Rachel, whom I had helped get a job, sent me a text: "Do you know what they call you behind your back here?" She was referring to the other servers, who just so happened to be a group of White girls. No, I replied. "MAN FACE." A couple months later, I turned in my kimono and jumped ship to the Applebee's down the road.

Changing restaurants, hell even changing industries, didn't change the fact that these kinds of things happened all the time. I was pretty, I was ugly, I was only successful because I had boobs. I was damned no matter what I did or didn't do. Part of the reason I wanted to get out of my sales role in the home warranty biz was because of how hyper-competitive some of the other reps became. Some of the guys were huge mudslingers and I didn't feel passionately enough about home warranties to play dirty with these fools. I had Realtors call me up, screaming at me about all the ways my company was screwing over their clients. Grown ass men throwing full-fledged temper tantrums, the likes of which put my ASD kiddo's meltdowns to shame.

I was belittled as a woman, since I had a husband who worked, so I didn't really need to and therefore my male counterparts "deserved" the business more than I did. I was told I must "do well" since I had such a pretty smile. Y'know, not because I busted my ass and worked really hard. All I had to do was smile and Voila! Money in the bank. Being a woman is so fun and easy!

Once, after I had gotten my eyebrows micro-bladed, I stopped by an office and the broker touched them— my EYEBROWS! —and marveled, "Oooh. You're tattooed." Um, yes, I am. But not on my face. No touchy. Commenting on (and touching!) physical attributes was practically the norm in the world of serving and bartending. I don't know why I expected any better in a more "professional" career. And if this sounds like an overreaction or dramatization, consider this situation if it involved touching a man's face. Can you imagine that? Because I can't. But honestly—the years of degradation only served as more fuel for my fire.

It's funny that I never realized I possessed "leadership attributes," even though I had been the drum major of my high school marching band and a trainer at many of the restaurants where I worked over the years. After I graduated college, I made a conscious effort to get involved with committees and organizations, and when there were opportunities to chair events, I decided to get out of my comfort zone and step up to the challenge. Basically, I invited myself to "The Table." Otherwise, I don't know that anyone would have asked.

In some of these leadership roles, I found a shortage of diversity so I stepped in to bridge that gap. I quickly discovered there were a lot of gaps to fill. In my own community the Hispanic population makes up nearly 33 percent of our residents, second to Whites at 61.4 percent. Those numbers don't correlate with our local organizations, businesses, and leaders. The category of "Two or more races" that I occupy is the third highest at 2.5 percent. I plan on taking up a lot of space in that arena. Blacks, Native Americans, and Pacific Islanders fill in the tiny remaining percent of the population.

I'm not saying my town is racist; I'm not saying minorities are being held back by White Supremacists; but I am saying that minority voices need to speak up, be seen, and be heard. There is a "Wall of Fame" at a local conference center that features forty years of people who have made great impact on the community—and every single face smiling from that wall is White. Surely I'm not the only one who notices this. If, all other factors being equal, that wall correlated to our demographics, thirteen of those photos *should* be a Hispanic face beaming proudly at the camera. Where is the ethnic diversity representation? Have no minorities made significant changes in the community in the last forty years?

As a speaker, I see all too often lineups that are all male and/or all White, both locally and even internationally. There's a whole phenomenon around "manels" and lack of diversity on stages. (It's a thing. Google it.) I went so far as to research speaker bureaus for women, Asians and Asian women. I actually found one based out of Singapore that I joined, just to share a sense of unity with like-minded women. I was once approached by the Black Speakers Network, which got awkward AF when I had to explain to them that I wasn't Black. My ethnicity is so enigmatic! I briefly considered pretending to be Black but didn't think that would end well, like the

1986 comedy *Soul Man*, where a White guy takes tanning pills to qualify for a scholarship for Black students.

I know my experiences are neither unique nor as bad as what many others experience. When I was in middle school in South Carolina, there was a big Black kid named Marlin who tormented me on the bus every day. He'd sit directly behind me and poke me, mimic me, and otherwise purposely get on my every damn last nerve. One day toward the end of seventh grade, I had finally had enough. As soon as the bus dropped us off at the school, I marched over to where he stood on the blacktop. Egged on by my friends, I pushed him and pompously said, "What are you gonna do now, nigger?"

As soon as that vile word passed over my lips, I knew it had been a mistake. Like when I found out years earlier that boys' private parts were tender, I wanted to hit this kid where it hurt. I knew the N-word would inflict some damage on him. I don't think it's possible to even say the word without an ugly sneer, and I felt hideous as the word spewed out of my mouth. I could have gone for his junk, but instead I went for his jugular.

I saw a fire ignite in his eyes and watched, as if in slow motion, as he raised his fist into the air and brought it down into my jaw, knocking me to the asphalt. Stunned, I laid on the ground for a minute, watching kids scatter quickly away from the scene of the crime. Someone helped me up and led me to the principal's office. I had never been to the principal's office for anything other than accolades and accomplishments. I was terrified to be headed there under the current circumstances.

Marlin was already in there, looking anxious and guilty. I knew he would be in trouble for hitting a girl, but I also knew I would be in possibly *bigger* trouble for calling him the N-word. Except when our principal, Mr. Sanders, asked about what had happened, Marlin didn't say anything about the N-word. I glanced sideways at him, wondering why he wasn't ratting me out. He could have very easily told Principal Sanders, who was in fact a Black man, exactly what I had said, and I probably would have received a much-deserved, harsh punishment.

I think he knew, at the young age of thirteen, that no matter what I had done to provoke him, the target on his back was much bigger than mine. That no matter the infraction, whatever the Black kid did would be worse than the half-breed Filipina. I felt indebted to him after that. He covered for me when he didn't have to. An unspoken pact formed between us that day, as we each exchanged wistful apologies. He stopped driving me crazy on the bus. We even became somewhat cordial with one another. Later, in high school, when we passed in the hallways, we'd give each other the "What Up" nod.

That experience served as a reminder to treat people with dignity, especially if it was someone bigger than me who could legit kick my ass. Seriously though, I never understood the hate people had for others based solely on skin color or gender or sexual preference. And I didn't hate Marlin because he was Black, I just wanted him to stop bullying me on the bus. I knew, as a byproduct of growing up in The South, that calling him a derogatory racial slur "put him in his place." It dehumanized him enough for me to feel like I was in the right and he was in the wrong. In short, it made me an asshole in that moment.

The dehumanization process creates a cultural chasm, placing groups into categories of "less than" and making connection nearly impossible. As Brené Brown wrote in *Braving the Wilderness:*

"Dehumanizing often starts with creating an *enemy image*. As we take sides, lose trust, and get angrier and angrier, we not only solidify an idea of our enemy, but also start to lose our ability to listen, communicate, and practice even a modicum of empathy."

I've been told I "make things about racism and sexism" anytime I mention the lack of diversity or the perceived different treatment I see as a minority woman. I've been told the Gender Pay Gap is a myth. I have quietly collected screen shots of all-White speaker lineups, a wall of fame, and other high-profile positions to someday serve as proof of the point I'm too scared to openly discuss, for fear of criticism and making something a big deal that isn't. Except it is.

I don't expect special treatment as a minority woman; I don't want to be a "Token" anything, simply checking off some boxes to fill a certain quota. And if I have to work twice as hard as my Caucasian male counterparts, I will. I have no qualms about having to hustle. But please don't insult me or any other marginalized group by implying that what is our reality is a non-issue. I admit, I see it more because I'm looking for it (thanks, Reticular Activating System!). But even if you don't see it or don't understand it or don't want to admit it: it's happening. As Brené wrote:

"When we engage in dehumanizing rhetoric or promote dehumanizing images, we diminish our own humanity in the process.

When we reduce immigrants to animals [like Trump did earlier this week], it says nothing at all about the people we're attacking. It does, however, say volumes about who we are and our integrity."

How much hurt could we cure with kindness? How much hate could we extinguish with empathy? It starts with us, with creating one small ripple. We all have the power to make massive positive change, starting with ourselves. Y'all remember the "Care Bear Stare"? Yeah, it's like that. In the immortal words of Bob Marley: "One Love. One Heart. Let's get together and feel all right."

THE END

"I hate goodbyes."
~Jim Carrey as Floyd, *Dumb and Dumber*

On July 30th, 2019, my ex-husband turned forty-three years old. He worked a long shift, as he always did, at his job as a produce manager at a local grocery store. After work, he came over to our house to pick up Haiden for a sleepover. With the promise of spaghetti for dinner and hours of Fortnite gameplay that he never got with us, Haiden happily gathered his iPhone, headphones, and Judy Hopps doll as he went with his dad for the much-anticipated festivities.

Dusty and Eli left to go play basketball at a friend's house, and I found myself gleefully, gloriously alone in the house for what seemed like the first time all summer. I cracked open a beer, a marathon-themed brew that tasted like post-run, sweaty socks wrung into a Michelob Ultra. I had bought a twelve-pack on a whim when I noticed it at a convenience store. After I tried the first one, I regretted that there were eleven more to go. But I'm not a wasteful person, so I chugged along, determined to eventually finish the remaining cans.

I opened up my laptop, excited to have some quiet writing time. I took a couple sips of the cringe-worthy beer and saw that an unknown number was calling my cell phone. Due to the high number of phone solicitations I receive, I let it go to voicemail and was surprised that whoever it was had left a message. I listened and re-listened as a man's voice explained that he was a detective, he was at my ex-husband's place, he knew my son was autistic, and he wanted to know if I could come get him.

A few short, but seemingly excruciatingly long, minutes later I arrived at the apartment complex where Haiden spent the night with his dad a couple times a month. Even though it was less than a mile from our house, I had never been there in the year his dad had lived there. He always came to our house to pick up or drop off Haiden, or we met at a predetermined location. I was filled with trepidation as I pulled into the unfamiliar parking lot and was greeted by three law enforcement officers. The one who had called me a few minutes earlier approached me and escorted me into the apartment building.

Haiden and his dad stood in the hallway outside of the apartment, along with a few more LEOs. I felt a major sense of alarm as I mentally calculated how many officers were there. Haiden was noticeably shaken, flapping his left hand and shifting back and forth on his feet. "Mom, I feel like there are butterflies in my stomach," he said when he saw me. "Me too, buddy," I soothed. "Me too." I looked at his dad, who wouldn't look me straight in the eyes. His face looked pale and ashen.

"Happy birthday," I said to him. "This doesn't look like the best way to celebrate."

He gave me an empty laugh and said, "I'm not sure why they seem so interested in my phone."

He tried to make light of what I knew in my gut was a very heavy situation. I asked one of the officers if I could take Haiden home. He said I could but Haiden told me he wanted his phone which he had left in his room. The officer said someone would get it for him but they needed the code so they could do a "precursory check" first. Haiden became even more agitated, confused about why they wanted to check his phone. I assured him he had nothing to worry about, but while we waited for them to check it out, he chattered anxiously about every random thing that seemed to pop into his mind in that moment. It's funny that, even though we hadn't done anything wrong, Haiden and I were so tense. I felt sweat drip down my bosom (#swoob) and my armpits. A beefy, tattooed officer standing nearby looked at me incredulously as he listened to Haiden rattle on and on about LEGOs and Fortnite and said, "Wow. This kid is awesome." I laughed nervously and agreed.

A few minutes later, someone handed Haiden his phone and told us we were free to go. Haiden hugged his dad and said, "I'll be back for spaghetti later." When we got into my car, I took a couple breaths to slow my rapid pulse. I didn't know much about legal proceedings, but it had seemed like a shit ton of cops at his place. I had a feeling that whatever was going down was not going to end well.

"Buddy," I said calmly, "I don't think you're going to be coming back tonight. I think your dad might be in some trouble."

Fortunately, I had the ingredients at home and I made spaghetti there. Then we watched a movie together. It was the summer of Marvel movies, so that night's choice was *Iron Man 3*. The entire time, I fought feelings of panic that rose in my chest like heartburn after a plate of spicy Mexican food. Later that evening, the detective called to tell me Haiden's dad had been arrested. He wasn't at liberty to discuss the details with me but I could find the charges on the website for the county jail. My heart sank and I wondered how the hell I was going to explain this to Haiden.

***

Just as that detective couldn't divulge details of the arrest, I'm not here to tell someone else's story. And, honestly, I don't know all the details myself except for what the charge is and how much the bail was set at. But having been married to him for almost five years and divorced from him for nearly eleven, I can say that the charges didn't shock me. Dusty and I dreaded the conversation we had to have with Haiden, not knowing how he would react to everything.

When Dusty told him the next day, he took it better than we thought he would, which we attributed to him not fully understanding the gravity of the situation. He was mostly concerned about when he would be able to play Fortnite again, since he only played it on the PlayStation 4 at his dad's place. And he was also worried about his bunny, Dan, who was in a cage in his bedroom at his dad's apartment.

'Shit!' I thought. I had completely forgotten about the bunny that Haiden's dad had gotten him a few months earlier. I started making frantic calls until I finally got it arranged to get the apartment keys from someone at the jail. Once I had those in hand, I was on Operation Rescue Dan Dan the Bunny Man. I took Haiden over to his dad's apartment so he could grab anything else of his that was there. Maintaining all semblance of structure and normalcy for Haiden became our main priority.

It felt eerie letting myself into someone else's private space, rifling around like some post-apocalyptic scavenger. Garbage bags filled the small entryway and a putrid smell hit my nose as soon as I stepped inside. It was disturbingly filthy, plates of uneaten leftovers on nearly every countertop, coffee table and dining table. Empty beer cans littered every room. Haiden's dad's bedroom floor wasn't even visible beneath the mountain of empty Bud Light boxes. Candy wrappers, empty chip bags, and wood shavings from the bunny's cage covered Haiden's floor. I found an empty box and filled it with the few belongings Haiden had there, as well as the PS4, grateful it hadn't been taken as evidence during the arrest. I grabbed the bunny's cage, piled everything outside the apartment door, and locked up the mess behind me. I had no idea how bad things were until that day, and I felt sick knowing I had let Haiden spend time in such a disgusting environment.

When I asked Haiden why he hadn't told me how dirty it was there, he replied, "You know I don't pay attention to my surroundings." And why would he, when he could sit in his bedroom, eating junk food and playing video games for hours on end? It was always important to me that Haiden have time with his dad and, in all honesty, it was a reprieve for me to have the occasional break too. But knowing now the situation over there, I felt a deep, sick guilt in the pit of my stomach. The feeling was exacerbated by some of the very straightforward and unfiltered things Haiden had to say about everything, such as:

"Maybe this wouldn't have happened if you hadn't broken up with dad."

"Why *did* you break up with dad?"

"He was just really lonely since it's been so long since you broke up with him."

"Well, have *you* ever done anything illegal?"

We knew we had to tread very lightly around the topic, so as to answer his burning inquisitions while keeping his dad perched, albeit somewhat precariously, on the pedestal on which he resided in Haiden's mind. For that first week after the arrest, I perpetually felt like I had just gotten off the Gravitron ride at the fair, nauseous and a little dizzy. I never could have prepared for the emotional toll this situation created in our already weird household.

Again, like when I had heard about Stacey's downward spiral years earlier, I felt like I was somewhat to blame. Maybe none of this would have happened if I hadn't left him. Then again, maybe this just solidified all the reasons I had.

Nearly a month after the arrest, the bail, initially set at $200,000, was reduced to $100,000; not that it mattered since neither he nor anyone else in his family could have afforded to bail him out, no matter how much it was reduced. Six figures, I thought. There are murderers whose bail is lower than that. What the hell did he do, exactly? I checked the website for the local paper multiple times a day, worried his arrest would make the news. We talked openly with Haiden about what we knew and told him he could ask us any questions. But then Dusty told him not to talk about it with anyone else outside of our family, to basically keep it a secret.

And there it was: that shameful silencing that I had grown to loathe from my own childhood (and even into my adulthood). Creating a stigma for Haiden, a certain burden of responsibility, for something he hadn't done wrong. Not that Haiden was some social butterfly with tons of people he would even tell; but now, just as easily as he rattled off anything and everything one ever needed to know about Nerf blasters, he would have to make the effort to not blurt anything out about his dad's current residence status. I'm sure Dusty had thought it was an innocuous enough request, but then I saw its impact on Haiden.

We had gone to a local hot air balloon festival that had been somewhat dramatic when Haiden had a meltdown as soon as we had parked the car. After nearly fifteen minutes, I managed to coerce him out of the car and then helped calm him down with an Italian ice at the festival. He got antsy waiting for the balloons to fill, so we walked around to check out some of the vendors. I was happy to see a familiar face, my friend Brian, who was a local Realtor. We joined him for a few minutes, sharing the kettle corn he offered and chatting about the goings on in each other's lives. Haiden hit it off with him and they talked about art, comics and copyright laws. Because why *wouldn't* they talk about copyright laws on a Saturday night? At some point, Haiden mentioned what a rough summer he had had.

"Why?" Brian inquired. "What happened this summer?"

I saw Haiden hesitate and then he looked at me.

"Is it okay if I tell him about dad?" he asked me.

"Of course it is," I said, somewhat surprised. This was the first time he had asked this question. Clearly, he felt that Brian was trustworthy enough for him to be comfortable sharing his secret. Brian was a cool grownup who conversed with him about topics that interested him. Haiden, who so often struggled with conversations, connected with him. It was fairly monumental. "If you want to talk about it, you absolutely can."

I could sense Haiden's relief. Brian, of course, was a total champ and listened without judgment. Later, on the car ride home, I told Haiden I was proud of him for talking to Brian, that I appreciated him asking for permission to talk about his dad, and that if he wanted to talk about it in the future with whomever he chose, that he could. It wasn't his place to be punished or penalized for his dad's decisions, and he didn't need to be complicit by keeping someone else's dirty secrets. This didn't need to be another of those things we don't talk about.

***

A few years ago, I took one of those free, online character assessments and was somewhat surprised when my number one strength was 'Honesty,' but mostly because 'Humor' was number five and I thought the two should have been switched. Not sure the algorithms that got to that conclusion, but y'all know the internet is never wrong. I didn't realize how accurate this whole honesty business was until I started sharing my story. Like the saying goes, "The truth will set you free." It has, it really has. I hope it does for you, too.

French author and Nobel Prize winner André Gide said, "It is better to be hated for what you are than loved for what you are not." It's what Brené Brown would call "Wholehearted Living." And it's what I refer to as "Embracing Your Inner Badass." It's living safe in the truth that you can be loved for all that you are, including the shameful, hurt, broken parts of yourself that you long ago shelved in the dark recesses of your heart and mind. If you dusted them off now, could you see them in a different light?

Hardships are inevitable. How we deal with those hardships is what makes or breaks us. I know I have been broken by my fair share of them, but eventually, I repaired myself. The broken parts are still there but, like the *kintsugi* bowl I made at the retreat for sexual abuse survivors, they are more beautiful when they are visible and not hidden. From pain comes purpose. What makes us weak makes us warriors, and from struggles come strengths. (Don't judge, y'all. I love alliteration!)

If there is nothing else I have learned in my journey, and that I hope you take with you in yours, is that you are more powerful than you know. You are capable of such greatness, and you can create a life of abundance. Your mind is capable of manifesting all the things you want. I wasn't ready to believe this eleven years ago, and I'd roll my eyes when people talked about their vision boards or the cheesy movie *The Secret*. I mean, I still think the movie is pretty cheese-tastic, but I also know the concepts are real as hell.

When I thought about what I wanted for the cover of this book, the image of a purple party dress came into my mind. I have always had a thing for purple; in high school I wanted a purple VW bug, I wore lots of purple clothes, wrote with purple pens, and even ordered an amethyst for my class ring because I hated my birthstone, garnet. Later, Mia was born in February and I was so glad to have more reason to wear amethyst. When I went to Weber State University, my fourth and final attempt at college, the school color was purple. The Younique Foundation that hosted the Haven Retreat I attended in March of 2018 also used the color purple as part of their brand. The Universe has surrounded me with purple for so much of my life.

So, it only seemed fitting for me to get a purple dress for this very important life occasion. I pictured the perfect dress: it had to be strapless, with a poofy tulle skirt, and less than $50. I immediately started an online search while lying in bed. The next day, I stopped by two consignment stores and left both, empty-handed, feeling discouraged. I didn't have a lot of time and needed to get home but I also felt compelled to try one last store. There was a Savers nearby so I decided to stop there really quick. When I walked in, I glanced at the little sign that listed that day's discounted color tag, which was blue. I headed over to the small section of secondhand formal dresses.

Hanging there, almost distanced from all the other dresses, was the dress you now see me wearing on the cover of this book. (You're looking at the cover now, aren't you? It's okay—go look.) The price tag listed the dress for $14.99—what a steal! But the tag was—you guessed it—blue. I manifested my perfect purple party dress for eight dollars. Y'all—this shit is real! I found it because I was looking for it. Who knows how long that dress hung there, passed up by others for one reason or another? Because it was meant to be there for me in that exact moment that I was looking for it.

And so it goes in life. You want to find your inner badass? The perfect person for you? Happiness? Success? Wealth? It exists and is going to be there when you're ready to find it. Don't believe me? If you're reading these words now, remember that not so long ago, these were ideas in my head. They were blank, nonexistent pages. On a whim one day, I opened up my laptop and started typing. I told people I was writing a book. And now, my dear friend, you have read the physical manifestation of my heart and my soul. Pretty trippy, right? And if I can do this, YOU can do whatever you were meant to do, too.

You and I: we are badass humans. Even if you don't like the word 'badass.' Hell, even if you don't like *me*. I'm okay with that—I'm not for everybody.

Hi, I'm Stacy and I'm a Recovering Nobody. And now? Now I'm a disruptor, a loud voice, a force to be reckoned with, an advocate, a champion for the underdog. I'm just one person trying to make a difference behind a long line of others who have laid the groundwork on which I am building. Want to join me? Want to be the change you wish to see in the world? You have it in you, whatever it is you set your heart and mind to do. It's a scary ride, but damn is it an adventure. Go share your story. Someone is waiting to hear it. Thank you for letting me share mine.

ABOUT THE AUTHOR

You just read over 60k words about the author, but in case you need a little more info, here you go:

Stacy Bernal is a speaker, trainer and author at See Stacy Speak LLC. She graduated Summa Cum Laude as the 2013 Outstanding Graduate of the Year in Public Relations and Advertising from Weber State University. She is actively involved in her community as an ambassador for the Ogden Marathon, a Women in Business executive, a member of Leadership Northern Utah, and a director for the WSU Alumni Association.

In 2018, she organized Ogden's first Autism Awareness walk which lead to the creation of Awesome Autistic Ogden the next year. In 2019, she founded the Bernal Badassery Foundation, a 501(c)(3) nonprofit, whose mission is to help families and individuals, both off and on the autism spectrum, who are working to better their lives and need a helping hand along the way. People who are "Badassery in Progress."

Stacy lives happily by the mountains where she enjoys all the outdoor recreation Utah has to offer, including trail running, mountain biking, swimming, and paddle boarding. She and her hubby Dusty balance the crazy shenanigans of the Bernal household, working hard to raise awesome humans, leave a legacy of positive change, and keep up with the piles of never-ending laundry.

Stacy has also gotten really good at writing about herself in third person.

If you are interested in booking Stacy for a speaking event, you may send an inquiry to stacy@seestacyspeak.com. For more info about Stacy (although, what more could you possibly need after reading this?), please visit:
www.seestacyspeak.com.

Made in the USA
Columbia, SC
30 November 2020